DATE DUE

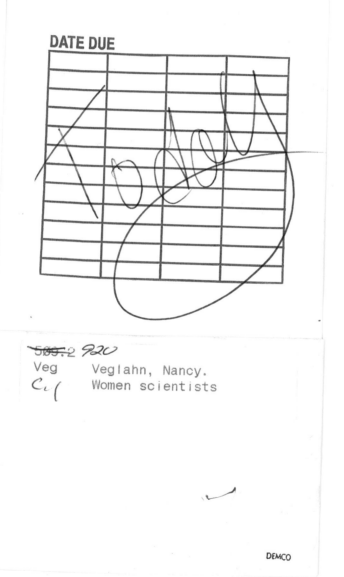

DEMCO

WOMEN SCIENTISTS

A M E R I C A N

P R O F I L E S

WOMEN SCIENTISTS

■

Nancy J. Veglahn

Facts On File, Inc.

Women Scientists Cv1 2000 11.19

Facts On File, Inc.
11 Penn Plaza
New York NY 10001

Library of Congress Cataloging-in-Publication Data

Veglahn, Nancy J.
    Women scientists / Nancy J. Veglahn.
        p.   cm. — (American profiles)
    Includes bibliographical references and index.
    Summary: Profiles the lives and achievements of ten American women
    scientists, including Annie Jump Cannon, Margaret Mead, and Rachel
    Carson.
    ISBN 0-8160-2482-0
    1. Women scientists—United States—Juvenile literature.   2. Women
in science—United States—History—Juvenile literature.
    3. Science—United States—History—Juvenile literature.   [1. Women
scientists.   2. Scientists.]   I.Title.   II. Series: American
profiles (Facts On File, Inc.)
    Q130.V44   1991
    509.2'2—dc20
    [B]
    [920]   90-26995

Facts On File books are available at special discounts when purchased in bulk quantities for businesses, associations, institutions or sales promotions. Please contact our Special Sales Department in New York at 212/967-8800 or 800/322-8755.

You can find Facts On File on the World Wide Web at http://www.factsonfile.com

Cover design by Matt Galemmo

Printed in the United States of America

MP FOF 10 9 8 7 6 5

This book is printed on acid-free paper.

Contents

Introduction   vii

Alice Eastwood   1

Nettie Maria Stevens   15

Annie Jump Cannon   26

Alice Hamilton   36

Edith Quimby   48

Gerty Cori   57

Margaret Mead   66

Barbara McClintock   78

Rachel Carson   92

Rosalyn Yalow   106

Mildred Dresselhaus   117

Index   129

Lilabeila

Introduction

*I*n his journal, the first governor of Massachusetts Bay Colony, John Winthrop (1588–1649), told of a Mrs. Hopkins who damaged her mind by reading and writing too much. He commented that if she had only tended to her housework instead of dabbling in "such things . . . [that] are proper for men, whose minds are stronger," she would not have suffered from such a breakdown.

During the first 100 years of the United States' history, there were no American women scientists. Like John Winthrop, most people believed not only that women had weaker bodies than men but that they also had weaker minds.

Females received only the most elementary education. The lucky ones were taught how to read and write and possibly to do some simple math. They also learned a bit about art and music, and some were taught a foreign language. The great universities such as Yale, Harvard, and Princeton were closed to them. It was thought that women did not need a college education. Their destiny was in the domestic arts and childrearing. College might even be harmful to their delicate systems—especially difficult subjects such as higher mathematics and science.

Without any education in such subjects, women could not become professional scientists. Some of those whose minds were inclined that way found uses for their neglected abilities. They studied wild plants and their uses or became expert gardeners. They invented gadgets to make their housework easier. They were midwives and unofficial doctors. These anonymous female scientists made great contributions to their families and communities, but they did not have the opportunity to win public recognition of their efforts.

Beginning early in the 1800s a few institutions of higher education for women only were established. But as long as women were educated separately, they had no chance to disprove the prevailing belief that they were mentally inferior to men. In 1833, Oberlin College in Ohio became the first to open its doors to women as well as men. The University of Iowa followed in 1856. Opportunities continued to expand through the rest of the 19th century. It was not until quite late in the 19th century, when a fair number of women had finally been admitted to American colleges and universities, that it became possible for a woman to earn her living as a scientist.

As more American women became educated, people began to realize that their mental abilities were equal to men's. A few male scientists with advanced ideas took a chance and hired female assistants. These women did so well that the old barriers gradually broke down.

The first science in which American women were able to make a mark was astronomy. Maria Mitchell (1818–89) discovered a new comet in 1847. She taught for many years at Vassar College, one of the new women's colleges in New York State. However, she was hampered all her life by poor laboratory equipment.

Gradually, women worked their way into jobs in other areas of science, especially biological and medical research. Most of these pioneering American women scientists remained unknown to the public. A few, through extraordinary talent and effort, made names for themselves in what had always been the domain only of men.

Of the 11 women profiled in this book, six were born in the 19th century and five in the 20th century. A comparison of these two groups helps to show the changes that have occurred during the last century.

The 19th-century woman had to choose between marriage and a career. Most chose marriage; relatively few careers were open to women anyway. Four of the six women born before 1900 remained single all their lives. Only two, Edith Quimby and Gerty Cori, were married, and these two were born in the 1890s. In contrast, three of the five scientists born in the 20th century married and had children.

In the late 1800s it was still hard for women to get a top-quality education in America. Only two of the six born in the 19th century earned Ph.D. degrees. One, Alice Eastwood, never went beyond high school. Of the later group only one, Rachel Carson, lacked a Ph.D. degree.

Even if she achieved something outstanding, it was unlikely that a woman scientist would get much recognition in the world of the 19th century. Nettie Stevens made an important discovery at the same time or slightly before a male scientist came to the same conclusion. He is the one who is remembered for that discovery. Gerty Cori and her husband worked together and published their results together; he alone won the Lasker Basic Medical Research Award. But 20th-century scientists such as Margaret Mead and Rachel Carson became world famous in their own right.

The 11 scientists described in this book had a variety of backgrounds. Alice Hamilton, Annie Cannon, Margaret Mead, and Gerty Cori were born to relatively well-off families and grew up in privileged circumstances. Alice Eastwood, Rosalyn Yalow, and Mildred Dresselhaus spent their childhoods in circumstances of severe poverty. Alice Eastwood and Gerty Cori were born in foreign countries and later became naturalized American citizens. Cori, Quimby, and Yalow worked closely with male partners, while Eastwood, Hamilton, Carson, and McClintock worked alone. The 11 worked in many different scientific fields, including astronomy, anthropology, botany, radiology, physics, electrical engineering, and cytogenetics.

Yet they also had much in common. All of them were, of course, exceptionally intelligent. They all possessed the kind of intellectual curiosity that a groundbreaking scientist needs. All these American women scientists wanted to make a contribution to the world they lived in and to those who would come after them. All of them had the self-discipline to carry through the detailed and challenging work they chose for themselves. And all 11 must have had unusually high self-esteem, for they had to struggle against prejudice and unequal opportunities. The odds were against their success, but they beat the odds in various ways.

Finally, the most important thing all of these women had in common was that each one achieved something outstanding in her branch of science. Some are remembered mostly for one breakthrough, a discovery that changed human thought and history. Some are known today more for long and productive careers than for any one accomplishment. But all of them deserve to be honored as outstanding scientists.

These are not the only American women who could have been profiled in a book like this. They were chosen because of the importance of their work and also to represent a variety of time periods and scientific fields. Here are a few others who could have appeared in this group:

Elizabeth Britton (1858–1934) was a botanist who specialized in mosses. Fifteen species of plants have been named for her. She and her husband were instrumental in establishing the New York Botanical Garden.

Eugenie Clark (1922–), an ichthyologist (expert on fish), became an authority on sharks and shark behavior.

Gladys Anderson Emerson (1903–) was one of the first biochemists to study the effects of vitamin E in the diet. She also did important work on the relationship between diet and cancer.

Helen Hyde (1857–1945), a physiologist at the University of Kansas, conducted research on the effects of radium and developed ways of investigating a single cell.

Helen Dean King (1869–1955), a biologist at the Wistar Institute of Anatomy and Biology in Philadelphia, published a great deal of research on the effects of close inbreeding in lab animals.

Helen Brook Taussig (1898–1986), a physician who was head of the Pediatric Cardiac Clinic of Johns Hopkins University's Harriet Lane Home, did important research on so-called blue babies. She helped to develop a surgical treatment for these children.

Margaret Floy Washburn (1871–1939), professor of experimental psychology at Vassar, published a book in 1908 called *The Animal Mind*, which has become a classic, and laid the groundwork for later studies of animal psychology.

Chien-Shiung Wu (1913–), a nuclear physicist, conducted experiments that helped to disprove what had been called a basic law of nature, the law of parity.

The lives of the 11 women included in this book cover a combined time period of more than 120 years. Three, Mildred Dresselhaus, Rosalyn Yalow, and Barbara McClintock, are still living and working. Most of them never knew each other. However, Edith Quimby was a mentor and role model for Rosalyn Yalow, and Rosalyn Yalow for Mildred Dresselhaus. Increasingly in the 20th century, established women scientists are able to help younger women develop their own careers in science.

Governor John Winthrop was wrong, of course, for none of these women or the other thousands of women scientists who have done important work in America seem to have "damaged" their minds by too much reading and thinking. Americans today are no longer wasting the talents of half the population because of such outmoded ideas.

Still, there is a lingering belief among some people that "math and science are not for girls." The following profiles of 11 women scientists show how false that belief is. As Nobel Prize–winner Rosalyn Yalow once said, "We still live in a world in which a significant fraction of people, including women, believe that a woman belongs—and wants to belong—exclusively in the home. . . . The world cannot afford the loss of the talents of half its people if we are to solve the many problems which beset us" (Vare, p. 132).

Alice Eastwood
(1859–1953)

This picture of Alice Eastwood was taken soon after she came to California.
(Courtesy Special Collections/Library, California Academy of Sciences)

A grove of redwood trees was named for her, and a building at the California Academy of Sciences, and a scholarship at San Francisco City College, and a rose-granite bench at the Shakespeare Garden in Golden Gate Park. But it was to flowering things that she devoted her life, and the flowers that bear her name are the most fitting memorials: *Eastwoodia*, a native California flower, and *Aliciella*, a desert flower, bloom every year in the West, living reminders of botanist Alice Eastwood.

1

Women Scientists

For more than 70 years, Alice Eastwood tramped through the western United States, climbing mountains, exploring deserts, sleeping out of doors when necessary, traveling on foot, on horseback, by stagecoach and train, and finally by car, in search of all the plants she could find growing in the wild. Between 1912 and 1949 she added 340,000 specimens to the herbarium at the California Academy of Sciences.

Alice Eastwood was born near Toronto, Canada, on January 19, 1859. She was only six when her mother, Eliza Gowdey Eastwood, died. Her father, Colin Skinner Eastwood, placed her and her younger brother and sister with relatives and went away. Although he kept in touch with the children, he could not afford to bring the family back together until eight years later. After several years at the home of an uncle, Alice and her younger sister were sent to live and attend classes at the Oshawa Convent in a nearby village. They were the only two boarding students there. Food was not plentiful, classes offered little to a bright girl like Alice, and the only books in the library were lives of the saints.

All her life, Alice Eastwood had an unusual ability to focus on essentials and ignore everything else. When she looked back on her childhood, she did not waste time whining about its hardships. Instead, she recalled how her uncle William Eastwood, an amateur botanist, generated her first interest in plants and gardens. She remembered Father Pugh, a retired priest who tended the gardens at the convent and allowed her to follow him and watch him work. She mentioned a nun who gave her a love of music.

Finally in 1873, when Alice was 14 years old, her father sent for her. He was living in Denver, Colorado, and her brother was already there with him. Alice took the long journey by train, earning her fare by taking care of a baby on the way. When she arrived in Denver she found that her father still did not have a place where she could live, but he had found her a job as live-in nursemaid to a wealthy cattleman's children.

The family she moved in with, the Scherrers, were kind to her, and she was delighted by their large library. Before long she found she could read while feeding the baby. That summer the Scherrers went camping in the high Rockies, and Alice went along. She was enchanted with the wildflowers and wanted to learn all their names. People in the area told her the common names of many varieties—Indian paintbrush, wild daisy, forget-me-not, iris, mariposa lily—but Uncle Eastwood and Father Pugh had taught her that each plant also had a proper botanical name. She decided she would have to get a book.

Alice Eastwood had found her life work. From that time on she never wavered in her passion for botany.

In the fall of 1873, her father built a store with living quarters in the back. Alice moved in, and eventually they were able to send for Kate as well. The children could all go to school now, but Alice and Kate were far behind grade level because of the inadequate education they had had at the convent. Alice did most of the housework, which meant spending her time after school cooking, cleaning, and washing clothes, as well as studying.

Then their father remarried. It was hard to include a new person in the family circle. Alice had been "mother" long enough to resent this stranger at first, but at least she now had a little more time to devote to schoolwork. Her father got a job as janitor at the new East Denver High School, and the family moved into the base-ment. They still had little money. Everyone had to help in order to take care of chores and pay the bills. Every afternoon, Alice and Kate helped their father clean the school rooms. Alice got up at 4:00 in the morning to stoke the furnace while her father and brother delivered newspapers. She also worked as a seamstress at a department store on Saturdays.

In the spring of 1878, Mr. Eastwood took Alice out of high school again because of financial problems. Alice worked full time but continued to study on her own, and she was able to pass a test to get credit for the school she had missed. In fact, she did better than pass: she scored 100. During all these years Alice somehow found time to read on her own as well. She loved the classic novels of Charles Dickens and Walter Scott but also discovered nature writers such as John Burroughs and Henry David Thoreau.

Because of the hodgepodge of schooling she had had, Alice was 20 years old before she graduated from high school in 1879. She was class valedictorian. This was the end of Alice Eastwood's formal education.

Even before graduation, Alice had been offered a teaching job at East Denver High School. To get a little experience in the classroom, she accepted a summer position at a small school 30 miles from Denver. She took along two treasured books, gifts from her teachers: *Flora of Colorado* and Gray's *Manual of Botany*. She learned to ride horseback as well as teach school that summer, and she began the long process of learning botany on her own.

In the fall she began teaching Latin to eighth graders at East Denver High. Her knowledge of Latin would be helpful for the rest of her life, since the botanical names of flowers and plants are always given a Latinate form. In the following years she taught many different subjects as well: drawing, astronomy, natural science, history, composition. In preparing for these classes, Eastwood continued the process of self-education that took the place of college and graduate school for her. Her salary of $50 a month sounds tiny today, but after years of real poverty it seemed adequate.

Summers were for botany. By making all her own clothes and spending money only for necessities, she was able to save enough during the school year to go to the mountains for the summer. She added a third book to her botanical library: Coulter's new *Manual of Botany of the Northern United States*. Venturing further each year into the remote parts of the Rockies, she patiently compared the plants she found to the illustrations and descriptions in her books until she knew the names of all the common flowers and shrubs and had identified many uncommon ones.

One advantage Alice Eastwood had was the fact that she had not been brought up as a "well-bred" young lady. No well-bred young lady in the 1880s would have traveled alone in the wilderness, sleeping out-of-doors at times or begging a room at isolated ranches, sometimes even traveling in the company of strange men. For that matter, it is unlikely that a well-bred young lady of that day would have been obsessed with the study of botany.

Not even the dress styles of the time could be allowed to hamper Alice's work. At first she made outfits that followed the styles of the day. But when the long, trailing skirts that were the fashion got in her way, she cut them off to ankle length. She rolled up her nightgown and stuffed it into the space where the bustle was supposed to be. Her shoes were sturdy and comfortable rather than dainty and fashionable. After a few years of riding sidesaddle, as ladies were supposed to do, she decided it was awkward and switched to a western saddle. She even invented a skirt for riding astride. It had buttons down front and back, so that it could quickly be converted to a sort of trouser.

Summer after summer, she went out beyond the last stops on the stagecoach lines, encountering rough frontiersmen, miners, Indians, cowboys, and wild animals along the way. She later said of those days: "Never in all my experience have I had the slightest discourtesy and I have never had any fear. I believe that fear brings danger" (Bonta, p. 10). Eastwood never carried a gun because she felt that would show fear.

Gradually her travels became known, and she developed a reputation as the local expert on Colorado wildflowers and plants. A member of the school board got her a railroad pass. By now, Eastwood was building her own *herbarium* (a collection of dried plants mounted and labeled for scientific study) of Colorado plants. The excitement of the chase grew every summer as she added more unusual specimens.

In 1887, a famous English botanist, Alfred Russel Wallace, came to Denver on an American tour. He wanted to climb Gray's Peak and asked for a guide with a knowledge of local plant life. One day in May the principal of her high school brought the tall, bearded Englishman to Alice Eastwood's classroom and introduced them. She recognized the name instantly. She had read his book, *Malay Archipelago*, and was familiar with "the Wallace Line," a theoretical dividing line between the plants of Asia and Australia.

That July they went together to climb Gray's Peak. Climbing up Grizzly Gultch, they stayed in a miner's hut above timber line. At 13,000 feet above sea level, it was said to be the highest dwelling in the United States. They spent three days there, happily gathering specimens of the wildflowers that grew so abundantly at the high altitude. In his autobiography, Wallace said that he found many new plants there and was most satisfied with the trip. Eastwood called it "a glorious adventure" (Bonta, p. 10).

She had other adventures in her explorations. She became friendly with Al Wetherill, the rancher who discovered the ancient Indian dwellings at Mesa Verde, and made several trips with him. Once they became lost, and he lowered her into a canyon and went off to find a trail. She spent the night on a ledge, then climbed down to the bottom of the canyon where he rejoined her with the horses. Still lost, they struggled on for another 24 hours before finding a trading post where they could get food and directions. Eastwood kept collecting all the way. For her, this trip was memorable because she found her first specimen of *Grayia brandagei* (a rare sage) and a *Gilia* she named *superba*. Much of Eastwood's work for the rest of her life involved *taxonomy*, the science of classifying and naming living things. The scientific name of a plant always consists of two words, the first being the name of the *genus*, or group to which it belongs, and the second being the name of the *species*, or particular member of the larger group.

Some small investments Alice and her father had made in Denver real estate began to pay off as the city grew. In the winter of 1890–91, Alice could afford to take a leave of absence from her teaching position and travel to California. She enjoyed a leisurely trip through the state, gathering plant specimens as she went, and eventually arrived in San Francisco where she wanted to visit the California Academy of Sciences. At the impressive new building on Market Street, she introduced herself to Townsend Stith Brandegee and his wife, Katharine, both of whom were well-known botanists. Katharine Brandegee asked Alice to write articles for the academy's natural history magazine, *Zoe*.

After 10 years of collecting, Eastwood had enough specimens to write a book. She called it *A Popular Flora of Denver*. Unable to find a publisher, she paid to have it printed. Despite its title, the book did not prove popular. There was no money to advertise it, and the book was a financial failure. Her father eventually became tired of the piles of leftover books and threw them away.

In 1892 Katharine Brandegee wrote to offer Alice Eastwood a job as joint curator of botany at the California Academy of Sciences. Alice hesitated. She loved Denver; her family was there; she had many friends in Colorado. But the opportunity was too good to pass up, so finally she donated her herbarium to East Denver High School, packed her bags, and boarded a train for California. (The herbarium was eventually passed on to the University of Colorado at Boulder and became the nucleus of their botanical collection.)

Within a year after her arrival in San Francisco, the Brandegees retired and moved away, and Alice Eastwood was named curator of botany. As a woman still in her thirties with only a high school education, she was head of a department in one of America's most important scientific institutions.

The academy sponsored education and research. Eastwood was used to teaching, so she did not find it difficult to take over the botany classes; it was a joy to teach only her favorite subject and to work with advanced students. She had also been doing research on her own for many years. Now she could use all her experience to make the academy a first-rate center for botanical information. She was to work toward that goal for nearly 60 years.

One of Eastwood's first tasks was to organize the large collection of plant specimens left by the Brandegees. These were piled here and there haphazardly; some were even beginning to mold in a damp corner. She patiently went through everything in the collection, marking each item with its botanical name, and devising more orderly ways to store and display the specimens.

She found new friends in San Francisco, young professional or amateur scientists who enjoyed going on outings on the weekends. They liked to explore the slopes of Mt. Tamalpais, cooking lunch over an open fire and then going off to look for birds, animals, rocks, trees, or flowers, as their personal interests dictated. They called themselves The Hill Tribe. Alice could outwalk, outclimb, and outcollect most of the others. When they could get a few weeks off they took longer trips, camping in the mountains.

These informal trips with friends did not provide enough specimens to fill up the academy collection as Eastwood wanted to do. She began traveling throughout California as she had Colorado, looking for plants that were not already represented in the herbarium. There were no automobiles or buses, no fast food restaurants, no motels. By train or stagecoach she got as close as she could to the area she wanted to explore, and then she set out on horseback or on foot, with a wooden plant press slung over her shoulder. In order to be preserved for study, the plants had to be dried in the sun and then flattened in the plant press until all moisture had been squeezed out.

After a dozen years of work, Eastwood had added thousands of items to the academy herbarium and had organized the collection carefully. She had even separated 1,497 of the most rare specimens from the rest, many of them plants that could not be replaced because they no longer existed as living organisms. She was soon to be grateful for that precaution.

On the morning of April 18, 1906, Eastwood woke early because her bed was shaking. The motion stopped after a few minutes, and she got up and made breakfast, assuming that this was just another minor California quake. But when she left home to go to work at the academy, she saw clouds of smoke over the city and people running through the streets. Her first concern was for the precious herbarium she had spent so many years tending.

She rushed to Market Street and, at first, thought the academy building was undamaged. But the doors were locked, and she could see fires creeping along Mission Street toward it. She managed to find one of her Hill Tribe friends, a lawyer named Robert Porter, and together they broke into the front hall of the academy. The hall was filled with rubble. The glass dome had shattered, and the marble staircase was in ruins. Her office and the herbarium were on the sixth floor.

The handrail still seemed to be firmly attached to the wall, so Alice and her friend decided to try to get to the upper floors that way. She hung her lunch bag on the horn of a stuffed mastodon in the hall, and they pulled themselves up six flights like mountain climbers, stepping on whatever fragments of the staircase projected from the walls.

There was no way the two of them could save everything. Eastwood spread her biggest work apron on a table, and Porter helped her fill it with the rare specimens she had separated from the main collection. They tied the bundle with rope, and Alice grabbed her favorite Zeiss lens and slipped it into her pocket. Then they climbed down the way they had come, getting out with the precious bundle just as flames began licking at the structure.

Five hundred people died in the San Francisco earthquake of 1906, and 250,000 were left homeless as fire destroyed four square miles of the city. The academy building was gutted. Almost all of the specimens Eastwood had laboriously gathered in California went up in smoke, along with all her records and almost all the copies of her second book, *A Handbook of the Trees of California*. Yet she was able to write in a letter to *Science* magazine just a month later: "My own destroyed work I do not lament, for it was a joy to me while I did it, and I can still have the same joy in starting it again . . . " (Wilson, p. 96).

But it would be a long time before she could start the work again. The academy was gone, and there was no money for rebuilding it. Eastwood put the specimens she had saved into storage and made her first trip to the East Coast. She had no job, no income except for the small amount of money her property in Colorado still earned, but by now she did have something more important: a reputation as one of the most knowledgeable botanists in the country. For several years she worked as a staff assistant at the Gray Herbarium in Cambridge, Massachusetts. She also spent time at the National Herbarium in Washington, D.C., meeting other botanists with whom she had been corresponding for years, and traveled to England to visit famous gardens there.

When Eastwood got back to the United States, she was greeted by a letter from the California Academy of Sciences. At last they were ready to rebuild in a new location—Golden Gate Park—and they wanted her to resume her position as curator of botany. She returned to California in the summer of 1912, rented one floor of a house where she could both live and work, and started gathering specimens to replace those lost in the fire. In the first summer she found 2,500 different plants. She also collected duplicates that could be traded to other museums for items the academy needed.

However, there was a limit to what she could do until the new building was completed. In 1914 she accepted the invitation of the Arnold Arboretum to go to the Yukon and study the willows in that region. She went by train to Seattle, then by boat to Skagway, train again to Whitehorse, then by stagecoach over the ice to Dawson. There she rented a miner's cabin that was heated by a woodburning stove made of an oil drum. A foot of ice covered the kitchen floor, so she cooked and ate in the living room. After several months in Alaska, Eastwood returned home, gathering plants all the way and drying them in the engine room of the boat.

Since the new academy building would be in Golden Gate Park, the park superintendent asked Eastwood to help plan the gardens and trees for the park. This job helped her to occupy her time while she waited for the building to be completed. She also went through all the books that had been given to the academy since the fire and organized a new library. At last the building was ready, and Eastwood could resume her old routine.

She thought the entrance hall of the new academy seemed rather drab, so in 1916 she began decorating it with flowers, changing the display every week. This made the building a popular San Francisco attraction. It became known as the longest-running flower show in the world.

By now Alice Eastwood was in her late fifties, an age when most people begin to look ahead toward retirement. She had no such thoughts and, in fact, was able to continue work at the academy for more than 30 years, retiring on her 90th birthday. During that time she built up the herbarium until it consisted of more than 300,000 items, published hundreds of scientific papers and articles on botany, and developed an outstanding library of rare botany books at the academy.

She became involved in many organizations such as the California Spring Blossom and Wildflower Association, the California Botanical Club, the American Fuchsia Society, and the Save-the-Redwoods League. She helped to plan the Shakespeare Garden in Golden Gate Park and also saw to it that the park was planted with a variety of trees and shrubs from all over the world. She became an expert on the history of botany as well, and published articles on the work of early explorers of the Pacific coast. She and her assistant, Tom Howell, started a quarterly magazine called *Leaflets of Western Botany*. At the age of 81 she went collecting with Howell in Death Valley.

One of the greatest thrills of her long life came in 1950, when she was named honorary president of the International Botanical Congress and flew to Sweden for the meeting. Eastwood loved to fly. Back in 1915 she had paid $5 for her first plane ride around San Francisco Bay; now at the age of 92 she took a commercial flight across the Atlantic Ocean. The meeting opened in the garden of Carolus Linnaeus, the 18th-century Swedish scholar who had created the modern science of botany. Eastwood was seated in the

Alice Eastwood at age 80, with plant specimens.
(Courtesy Special Collections/Library, California Academy of Sciences)

wooden chair that had belonged to Linnaeus, and she was recognized by scholars from all over the world.

Alice Eastwood died in 1953 at the age of 95. Still active until the last few weeks of her life, she never lost the zest and vitality that characterized her personality. The last thing she said to her biographer, Carol Wilson, was that "there is a part of me that will not die" (Wilson, p. 222).

In 1938, Eastwood posed beside Eastwoodia elegans,
a plant that was named for her.
(Courtesy Special Collections/Library, California Academy of Sciences)

No revolutionary scientific breakthrough created Alice Eastwood's reputation. She earned her place in the history of science in America through many years of painstaking scholarship and exhaustive field work. She was the only woman whose name was starred for distinction in every volume of *American Men of Science* published during her lifetime. She built, not once but twice, a major botanical collection at the California Academy of Sciences. Through her writing and the flower shows, she helped to popularize the study of botany. She helped raise public awareness of the need for conservation to save native American species. She encouraged amateur gardeners to experiment with unusual species. A skilled taxonomist, she added much to the knowledge of plant life, especially that which is native to Colorado and California.

In spite of all her other accomplishments, Alice Eastwood always remained what she had been at the age of 20: a teacher. Her successor at the academy, J. T. Howell, said that "No member of a botany class or garden club ever heard Miss Eastwood refuse to examine a plant with the disparaging remark, 'Oh, I've seen that flower before'" (Dakin, n.p.). She looked at each specimen presented to her as if she had never seen it before, identified it carefully, and used it to demonstrate the lessons she wanted to teach. This had to do with more than simply naming plants correctly. One of her favorite writers was Ralph Waldo Emerson, and she was careful not to become the sort of scientist he described in poetry, who "Love not the flower they pluck, and know it not, And all their botany is Latin names."

Alice Eastwood loved the flowers she plucked. It was that deep love of her lifework that enabled her to accomplish so much.

Chronology

January 19, 1859	Alice Eastwood is born near Toronto, Canada
1865	mother, Eliza Gowdey Eastwood, dies
1869	Alice moves into Oshawa Convent
1873	moves to Denver to join father and brother
1879	graduates from East Denver High School as valedictorian
1887	Alfred Russel Wallace visits Denver
1890–91	Eastwood makes first trip to California
1892	is named assistant curator of botany, California Academy of Sciences; first book, *A Popular Flora of Denver*, is published
1893	Eastwood is named curator upon retirement of Katharine Brandegee
1906	earthquake and fire destroy academy building
1911	Eastwood travels to England and France
1912	is rehired as curator of botany for new academy
1914	does research in the Yukon
1916	begins decorating new academy building with flowers each week
1929	John Thomas Howell hired as assistant
1949	Eastwood retires at age 90
1950	is named honorary president of the seventh International Botanical Congress; flies to Sweden
October 30, 1953	Eastwood dies of cancer in San Francisco

Further Reading

Bonta, Marcia. "Alice Eastwood." *American Horticulturist*. October, 1983, pp. 10–15. An interesting biographical sketch, illustrated.

Dakin, Susanna Bryant. *The Perennial Adventure*. San Francisco: California Academy of Sciences, 1954. Tributes to Eastwood collected and published shortly after her death; includes a brief overview of her life and career.

Hollingsworth, Buckner. *Her Garden Was Her Delight*. New York: Macmillan, 1962. This biography was written for adults, but the reading is not difficult. Includes a bibliography.

Ogilvie, Marilyn Bailey. *Women in Science*. Cambridge: MIT Press, 1986, pp. 51–52. A profile of Eastwood is included in this collection of brief biographies of women scientists who lived and worked before the 20th century.

Wilson, Carol. *Alice Eastwood's Wonderland: The Adventures of a Botanist*. San Francisco: California Academy of Sciences, 1955. This official biography is based partially on interviews with Eastwood.

Nettie Maria Stevens
(1861–1912)

Nettie Maria Stevens in 1904.
(Photo courtesy of Carnegie Institution)

Girl or boy? Nowadays, couples awaiting the birth of a child often know which it will be. Through the techniques of modern medicine, the sex of a baby can be discovered months before it is born, but during most of human history this was not so. Nor did people understand how a baby came to be one sex or the other.

In many past civilizations, a baby's sex was thought to be determined by the mother, since the baby developed in the mother's body. Sons were usually wanted more than daughters, because in many cultures sons would help support the family, while daughters married and went away. Wives who did not produce sons might be blamed for having only daughters.

As modern science developed, people began to understand more about the beginnings of new life. The invention of the microscope allowed scientists to study tiny pieces of tissue and to see how living things reproduced themselves. But even with all the new knowledge, at the end of the 19th century no one was sure how a child came to be born male or female. It was Nettie Maria Stevens, high school teacher turned *cytologist* (one who studies cells), who in 1905 deciphered the clues that answered this ancient question.

Nettie Maria Stevens was born on July 7, 1861, just at the beginning of the Civil War, in Cavendish, Vermont. Her father, Ephraim Stevens, was a carpenter and general handyman whose family had lived in New England for five generations. Julia Adams Stevens, her mother, died when Nettie was only two years old. In 1865 her father remarried, and Nettie and her sister, Emma Julia, were raised by a stepmother. Three brothers died in childhood.

The family moved to Westford, Massachusetts, where Nettie and Emma went to the public elementary school and then to the Westford Academy. They were lucky to grow up in a time and place where girls could get more than a basic "three Rs" education. Just after the Civil War, many new and old schools opened their doors to female students. The charter of the Westford Academy said that it was "free to any nationality, age, or sex" (Ogilvie and Choquette, p. 294).

From the beginning, Nettie Stevens was an outstanding student. She and her sister made nearly perfect grades at the academy. They studied English, Greek, Latin, writing, math, geography, logic, sciences, and music. Nettie especially liked geometry and other mathematics courses.

After graduating from the Westford Academy in 1880, Nettie became a teacher. She had all the education women in those days could expect to get; in fact, she'd had more than most. Now her family expected her to use that education to support herself until she married. Only a few occupations were open to women then: mainly teaching, nursing, and secretarial work. Nettie got a job at a high school in Lebanon, New Hampshire.

But she had not learned everything she wanted to know, and she knew she would not be content to spend her life as a high school teacher. During the three terms when she taught Latin,

English, math, and science in Lebanon, she saved her money; she was going to get more education.

As soon as she had enough money put away, Nettie Stevens enrolled at the Westfield Normal School (a teachers' college) in Westfield, Massachusetts. She got the highest scores on the entrance exams of any student in her class and went through the four-year course in just two years. Once again, she made top grades, with perfect scores in geometry, chemistry, and algebra.

Nettie also enjoyed college activities. She was a debater, belonged to a social club, and played the piano.

It was probably during her years at Westfield that Nettie Stevens began to dream of working as a research scientist. She was especially fascinated with laboratory courses in which she could use a microscope to study tiny living things that could not be seen with the unaided eye.

Microscopes were not really new, even in Nettie Stevens' day. At least 3,000 years ago, engravers used glass containers filled with water to magnify the surfaces they worked on. People began to use glass lenses for magnification around A.D. 1200, and the first form of the modern microscope was invented in about 1590. However, these early microscopes were crude. It was not until the 1800s, when much better glass-making methods were discovered, that really efficient microscopes could be made. The first American microscopes were produced in Canastota, New York, in 1838.

So in a way, the microscope offered a gateway to a whole new world—one that had been there all along, but invisible to the human eye. Nettie Stevens had the curiosity of a scientist, and it is not surprising that she was attracted to a science in which important discoveries were being made because of new technology. As scientists examined human blood under the microscope, they could see the bacteria and viruses that cause disease. As they looked at bits of skin and bone, they began to understand what the human body is made of and how injuries heal. As they observed tiny plants and animals, they learned much about all living things and the patterns of growth and decay.

Nettie Stevens graduated at the top of her class of 30, but Westfield Normal School seemed to be the end of the educational line for her. She had earned a teaching certificate, but in order to do graduate work she would first need a bachelor's degree. Most of the universities still did not admit women; and, in any case, she did not have the money to go on to one of the few universities that did admit women for advanced work. Once again, the natural thing was to find a teaching job where she could at least use the education she'd already gotten.

Nettie Stevens in 1880, as a new graduate of Westford Academy.
(Photo courtesy of Bryn Mawr College Archives)

For most of the next 13 years, Nettie Stevens worked as a teacher and librarian in Massachusetts. From 1884 to 1892 she was on the faculty of the Westford Academy, her alma mater. She also served as assistant principal of Howe School, in Billerica, Massachusetts. She earned a reputation as an efficient, well-liked teacher and administrator. Her specialty was, of course, the sciences—especially biology. But all this time, she was saving her money and looking ahead to the time when she could go back to school.

That time finally came in the fall of 1896, when she entered Leland Stanford University in California. She had to start out as a "special student" because of gaps in her earlier education and because of the long time that had passed since her graduation from the teachers' college. By 1897 she had done well enough to be admitted as a regular student, and three months later she was given advanced standing.

Stanford was an exciting school, with some of the best young professors in the country and a reputation for trying educational experiments (such as admitting women). Nettie must have had some worries at first, entering the program as a middle-aged "old maid schoolteacher" and taking classes filled with bright young men from top schools. But she had not been idle in the years since her graduation from Westfield Normal School. Teaching the sciences had given her a solid grasp of the basics. She had never stopped studying on her own, and she had great mental powers.

Stevens took much of her graduate work under Dr. Frank Mace MacFarland, who encouraged her interest in microscopic studies of small plants and animals. Dr. MacFarland spent his summers doing research at the Hopkins Seaside Laboratory in Pacific Grove, California, and he took Nettie Stevens along as an assistant. She was able to spend four summers working at Hopkins.

Because she could apply some of her credits from Westfield Normal School to her program at Stanford, Stevens earned a B.A. degree in just three years. She stayed on to work toward a master's degree. In 1899 her father and her sister, Emma, came to California to join her, and they found a place to live together in Mountain View, about five miles from the campus. Nettie commuted to Stanford by train and horse-and-buggy. She spent her last year there working on a master's thesis, "Studies on Ciliate Infusoria" (a report on her research with certain microscopic creatures). The first scientific paper she published was based on the thesis.

Stevens received her M.A. from Stanford in 1900 but still was not satisfied with the extent of her education. She returned to the East Coast to enroll as a graduate student at Bryn Mawr College near Philadelphia. Founded in 1880, Bryn Mawr was one of the new women's colleges that had been established in the East after the Civil War. Its faculty included two well-known biologists, Thomas Hunt Morgan and Edmund Beecher Wilson.

Nettie Stevens did such brilliant work in her first year as a graduate student at Bryn Mawr that Professor Morgan helped her to get a fellowship for study abroad. In 1901–02 she studied at the Naples, Italy, Zoological Station and at the Zoological Institute at Wurzburg, Germany. In Germany she worked in the laboratory of Professor Theodore Boveri, who was doing research on the role of chromosomes in heredity. Chromosomes are tiny threadlike structures found in each living cell, usually in the nucleus. Boveri and other scientists suspected that chromosomes carried the messages that determined the inherited characteristics in all plants and animals.

The work Stevens did in Germany helped prepare the way for her later contributions to science. Professor Morgan had also done research in Wurzburg, and he, too, benefited from that experi-

Nettie Stevens working at the Stazione Zoologica in Naples, Italy.
(Photo courtesy of Bryn Mawr College Archives)

ence. Later, Professor Boveri came to resent both Morgan and Stevens because of the papers they published based to some extent on work in his lab, calling them "bloodsuckers." Boveri had grown up in a time when individual scientists working alone could still make important discoveries that would make them famous. Increasingly in the 20th century, science was becoming so complex that cooperation and collaboration were replacing this older attitude. Nettie Stevens always saw herself as part of a team and never attempted to get the sole credit for her most important discovery.

Stevens was awarded her Ph.D. at Bryn Mawr in 1903. She then contacted the Carnegie Institute in Washington, D.C., in hopes of getting a grant to support her as a researcher. Professor Morgan had invited her to work with him in a study of the behavior of chromosomes in aphids (small, soft-bodied insects). In a letter of recommendation, Morgan praised her "independent and original mind." Professor E. B. Wilson's letter said she was "not only the best of the women investigators, but one whose work will hold its own with that of any of the men of the same degree of advancement" (quoted in Ogilvie and Choquette, p. 300).

While she waited for news on the grant, Stevens had a one-semester appointment as a research fellow at Bryn Mawr. However, she worried about the future as the months went by and she got no word from Washington. If she did not get the Carnegie grant, she knew she would have to find a teaching job and would probably have to forget about a career in research.

Finally, in March of 1904, Stevens learned that the Carnegie Institute had appointed her to one of its research assistantships. For a short time at least, she would have the freedom to do original research, seeking answers to some of the most basic questions of human existence.

She based her work on a study of a creature called *Tenebrio molitor*, or the common meal worm. Examining the cells of these invertebrates under her microscope, she discovered that the males produced two different kinds of reproductive cells, one with a large (X) chromosome and the other with a smaller (Y) chromosome. The unfertilized eggs of the female, however, always carried two X chromosomes. Her studies caused Stevens to conclude that if an egg were fertilized with a cell carrying the X chromosome it would produce a female, but if it were fertilized with a Y-chromosome cell it would produce a male.

Stevens reported her findings to the Carnegie Institution in 1905, as one of the conditions of her grant. The paper she sent them, titled "Studies in Spermatogenesis with Especial Reference to the 'Accessory Chromosome,'" was published as Carnegie Institution Publication No. 36, part one. It may have been the first scientific paper to correctly explain how gender is determined.

Professor Edmund B. Wilson, who had previously been on the faculty at Bryn Mawr and knew of Stevens's and Morgan's work, was doing similar research at the same time. He happened to be on the advisory committee that reviewed Stevens's paper for the Carnegie Institution. She submitted her paper to the committee on May 23, 1905. Wilson wrote a paper that was dated May 5, 1905, and published in August, which reached essentially the same conclusions. It is Wilson who is usually credited with this discovery.

Probably the two scientists, working independently, learned the same thing at about the same time. They both continued to footnote their own work with references to each other's research, and neither ever tried to get sole credit as the unraveler of the mystery of sex determination.

However, Stevens's first paper was more specific than Wilson's in drawing conclusions from the research. Wilson's first paper on the subject still allowed for environmental influences having some effect on the gender of an offspring. It was not until his second paper was published in October that he fully accepted the idea of chromosomes as the sole determiner of sex.

Other scientists were even slower to change their minds. Thomas Hunt Morgan, who had worked with Nettie Stevens at Bryn Mawr, continued to be skeptical for several years. In December of 1906, the American Society of Naturalists had a symposium on the subject at Columbia University. Morgan's paper argued that sex was determined as the fertilized egg developed, and that other factors such as the size of the egg played a part in making the individual male or female. It was not until 1910 that Morgan accepted the "accessory chromosome" theory.

Meanwhile, Nettie Stevens went on with her work. During the next six years she confirmed her findings by studying aphids and more than 50 species of beetles. A paper she published in 1905 on the life cycle of aphids won her the $1,000 Ellen Richards Prize, an award given by a group interested in promoting scientific research by women. Stevens also spent several summers as a researcher at the biological laboratory at Cold Spring Harbor, Long Island, New York.

She continued to teach at Bryn Mawr as well. Stevens was known as an outstanding teacher who took an interest in the progress of each of her students. When one former student hesitantly wrote her a letter inquiring about some biological questions, Stevens replied: "How could you think your questions would bother me? They never will, so long as I keep my enthusiasm for biology; and that, I hope, will be as long as I live" (Ogilvie and Choquette, p. 373). For many years after her death, her favorite microscope, which she willed to the Bryn Mawr biology lab, was known as "the Nettie Maria."

Nettie Stevens developed breast cancer and died of the disease on May 4, 1912, at the age of 51. The career that had begun so late in her life was cut short. There is no way to know what else this brilliant woman might have contributed to human knowledge if she had been able to work as a researcher for 30 or 40 years. However, in less than a decade she made a major discovery.

While Stevens cannot be called "the" discoverer of the chromosomal determination of sex, she is certainly one of the two discoverers of this significant fact. It was she who first clearly stated it, and she who was first convinced that chromosomes alone cause an offspring to be male or female. One biographical sketch of Stevens's life suggests that Wilson was eventually given the credit "because of his more substantial general contributions" (Ogilvie and Choquette, p. 292).

Wilson was able to make these "more substantial contributions" in part because he had a much longer career as a biologist. It is interesting to compare his life with Nettie Stevens's. Born five years earlier than she was, Wilson earned a Ph.B. (Bachelor of Philosophy) at Yale in 1878 and a Ph.D. at Johns Hopkins in 1881. By 1891, when Nettie was just starting her college work at Stanford, Wilson was a professor at Columbia. He eventually became chairman of his department there, and he continued to work as a teacher and researcher until many years after Stevens's death. Thomas Hunt Morgan came to Columbia to work with him, and these two men and their associates made many important discoveries related to genetics in the early part of the 20th century.

In spite of her genius and her hard work, Nettie Stevens never gained the prominence of scientists such as Wilson and Morgan. She simply started too late and died too soon. On the other hand, she had opportunities that were not available to her mother's and grandmother's generations. She did have the chance to use her abilities to make an exciting discovery.

Chronology

July 7, 1861	Nettie Maria Stevens is born in Cavendish, Vermont
1863	mother dies
1880	Stevens graduates from Westford Academy
1883	graduates from Westfield Normal School
1883–96	works as a teacher and librarian
1899	receives B.A., Stanford University
1900	receives M.A., Stanford University
1901–02	studies in Europe at Naples, Italy, Zoological Station and Zoological Institute, Wurzburg, Germany
1903	receives Ph.D., Bryn Mawr College
1904	receives research grant from Carnegie Institution
1905	publishes paper on sex determination; receives Ellen Richards Prize
1905–12	serves as associate professor, Bryn Mawr
May 4, 1912	dies of cancer

Further Reading

Ogilvie, Marilyn Bailey, and Clifford J. Choquette. "Nettie Maria Stevens" (1861–1912). *Proceedings of the American Philosophical Society*, Vol. 125, No. 4, August, 1981, pp. 292–311. Although some of the material on Stevens's work may be too technical for young readers, this article also gives an excellent account of her life.

Ogilvie, Marilyn Bailey. *Women in Science*. Cambridge: MIT Press, 1986, pp. 167–169. Offers short profiles of many pre-20th century American women scientists, including Stevens.

Ris, Hans. "Nettie Maria Stevens." *Notable American Women*. Cambridge: Harvard University Press, 1971, pp. 372–373. This is a good source of basic information about Stevens's life and work.

Vare, Ethlie Ann, and Ptacek, Greg. *Mothers of Invention*. New York: William Morrow, 1988, pp. 213–214. Stevens is one of many women whose accomplishments are briefly noted in this book.

Annie Jump Cannon
(1863–1941)

Annie Jump Cannon classified more than 350,000 stars during her lifetime.
(Photo courtesy Harvard College Observatory)

*M*ost 19th-century mothers taught their daughters to sew or draw or play the piano. Annie Cannon's mother took her to the attic at night to watch the stars. Using an old astronomy textbook as a guide, the two of them would peer out into the darkness and try to identify as many stars as they could. Mary Elizabeth Jump Cannon, Annie's mother, had learned to love star-gazing in her own childhood, and she passed that interest on to her daughter. As soon as Annie was old enough to stay up after dark and crawl through the trapdoor to the attic, she began going there on clear nights with her mother. Before long she had committed to memory a detailed map of the night sky, a map that changed with seasons but always in predictable ways. Her life's work began with this early training.

———

Annie Jump Cannon was born on December 11, 1863. Her father, Wilson Lee Cannon, was a shipbuilder in Dover, Delaware. Also strongly interested in politics and government, Wilson Cannon had been lieutenant governor of Delaware when the Civil War broke out in 1861 and had cast the vote that kept Delaware in the Union.

Mary was Wilson Lee Cannon's second wife. His first wife had died leaving four children, Annie's stepbrother and stepsisters. Mary Cannon took on heavy responsibilities when she married, and after Annie's birth she had two more daughters. Studying the stars relaxed her and let her forget her duties for a while. By the time Annie and her mother began their nightly starwatching, the war had ended and the shipyards were booming. Annie had a comfortable childhood as a member of a large and prosperous family. Her future seemed obvious: she would have a little basic education, marry, and raise a family.

Annie's teachers at the Wilmington Conference Academy made a slightly different suggestion to her father. She was an exceptional student, especially in math, and had a quick memory for the most detailed information. They thought she should have the chance to go to college. Several women's colleges had recently been founded in New England, and Annie's parents could afford to send her to one. There would be plenty of time for her to settle down as a wife and mother after some further education.

Wilson Cannon had married an intelligent woman and saw no reason why his bright daughter should not make use of the new opportunities for women to train their minds. He got information on all the women's colleges and decided that Annie should go to Wellesley College in Massachusetts. Open for only five years, Wellesley had already earned a reputation as one of the top academic institutions for women in the United States.

Annie left Delaware for Wellesley in the fall of 1880. She loved her classes and new friends at Wellesley, but she was not prepared for the New England winter. The clothes she had brought from Delaware offered only flimsy protection from the icy winds and snow. Her thin shoes let in the cold and damp, and her lightweight coat left her shivering after a walk across campus. She had one cold after another that first winter in Massachusetts. The constant coughing and repeated infections damaged her eardrums, leaving her partially deaf—a condition that grew worse later in her life.

Annie's favorite teacher at Wellesley was Sarah F. Whiting. Professor Whiting taught physics and other science courses, and she also worked in a little astronomy on the side. There was no observatory at Wellesley at that time, so there were no formal classes in astronomy, but Whiting took her students out onto a porch roof to see the great comet of 1882. (A comet is a heavenly body thought to be made up of ice, gasses, and dust from outer space. It looks like a star with a tail.) She also interested Annie in *spectroscopy* (using an instrument to study waves of light or energy). Inside the spectroscope was a glass *prism* (a solid object with triangular bases and rectangular sides). When light passed through the prism, it was separated into bands of different colors and lengths. These bands are called a *spectrum*. No two light sources have exactly the same spectrum, so the spectroscope offers an excellent way to study and identify stars.

In 1884, Annie graduated from Wellesley and returned home. While she had been away at college, many of her former friends had married and started their families. Older than most of the single women in her social set, Annie had also had more education. Although she was attractive and popular, she did not entirely fit in. Being hard of hearing must have made social situations somewhat difficult for her. She did not show much interest in any of the young men who were still "available" in Dover.

But if she did not marry, what was she to do with the rest of her life? Her family had enough money so that she did not *need* to work, and she did not feel inclined to follow the few occupations that were open to "respectable" women—teaching, office work, owning a dress shop. She enjoyed reading, cooking, and playing the piano, but these activities were not enough to fully occupy her time. She grew restless and bored. Not even the trip to Europe that she took in 1892 could make her content with her situation.

Then, in 1893, her mother died. Up to that time Annie had at least felt she was of some use in helping to run the household, and she had always enjoyed her mother's companionship. Suddenly the house in Dover became unbearable. Annie wrote to Sarah Whiting, her former professor at Wellesley, asking whether there might be some kind of position open at the college. Professor Whiting immediately hired Annie as her assistant. In addition to these duties, Annie was able to take graduate work in physics, math, and, at last, in astronomy, which was now offered at Wellesley.

Far from satisfying her, these further studies only whetted her appetite for more. Students at Radcliffe, the women's college at Harvard in Boston, Massachusetts, had access to Harvard's observatory. Radcliffe could therefore offer much more sophisticated classes in astronomy than those at Wellesley. In 1895, Annie Cannon enrolled as a special student in astronomy at Radcliffe.

At about the same time, Edward C. Pickering, the director of the Harvard observatory, got angry with a young man who was his student assistant. He announced to the unfortunate student that his Scottish maid could do a better job than he (the student) could. To prove his point, Pickering hired the maid, Wiliamina Fleming. She learned so quickly and did so well that he decided he would hire only female assistants from that time on. Pickering believed that the women were better observers than were most men, more patient with detail, and better able to adjust delicate instruments with their smaller hands and fingers.

Annie Cannon was the next young woman to benefit from Dr. Pickering's preference for female assistants. He hired her in 1896, and she was to spend most of the rest of her life working at the Harvard observatory.

Until the middle of the 19th century, astronomers had based their science entirely on observations of the night sky through telescopes. This meant that they could not work during the daytime or on cloudy nights. Much valuable time was wasted waiting for nights with perfect conditions; then when such a night did come along they had to work feverishly to make the most of it.

With the invention of photography, these limitations could finally be overcome. Pictures could be taken through telescopes on clear nights and studied later. Annie Cannon had begun learning about photography on her first trip to Europe a few years earlier. She had taken many pictures using a process with glass plates and developed the photographs herself. This knowledge would now come in handy. So would her training with the spectroscope. Dr. Pickering and his assistants were beginning to take spectroscopic pictures of the stars by equipping a telescope with a prism. The pictures produced in this way were called *spectrograms*. Instead of showing stars as people see them, they showed the differing bands of light produced by each star, providing a scientific way to tell one star from another.

When Annie Cannon went to work at the observatory, Pickering had already collected 10 years' worth of spectrograms. He planned to produce a catalog of the stars, based on this information. The catalog was to be named after Henry Draper, a pioneer in the development and use of the spectroscope. By this time some of the brighter stars had been described and grouped under alphabetical headings according to their brightness and other factors: A, B, C, and so on.

Cannon's job had two parts. First, she had to identify each star and describe it according to its spectrum; that is, she had to specify how this star was different from all other stars in the universe. Then she had to put that particular star in a group with other stars that were like it in many ways. This second step is called *classification*. It is a sorting process, like putting people into groups according to age, height, weight, hair color, and so on.

She quickly found that the original A, B, C groupings would not do for all the stars she was studying. Creating new groups and rearranging others, she finally came out with a system that went O, B, A, F, G, K, M, R, N, S. This sequence has been used ever since. It was hard for astronomy students to remember until someone came up with a sentence to help: "Oh, Be A Fine Girl, Kiss Me Right Now, Sweet." By 1910, Cannon's system of classifying the stars according to surface temperatures had become standard practice among astronomers everywhere.

During her first years on this project, Cannon worked mostly with *variable* stars, that is, stars that give off an unsteady light. These were hard to classify properly because the intensity of their light is different at different times. They remained Annie Cannon's favorite stars, perhaps because of the challenge they offered.

Annie Jump Cannon earned her M.A. degree from Wellesley in 1907. In 1911, she was named curator of photographs at the Harvard observatory, a title she would hold for the next 27 years. The job she had taken on required a lot of time and a great deal of patience. Day after day she studied her spectrograms; night after night she used the telescope to check her findings. Incredibly, she never tired of this enormous task. When asked how she could look at those peculiar streaky pictures constantly, she replied: "They aren't just streaks to me. Each new spectrum is the gateway to a wonderful new world" (Emberlin, p. 17).

This was work that required good eyesight, an enormous memory, and patience—qualities that Annie Cannon had. She also had great powers of concentration. Perhaps her deafness actually helped her here. She was not distracted by all the noises around her, and the stars make no sounds that humans can hear. Experience with the pictures increased her speed in interpreting them. By 1913 she could "do" three stars a minute from spectrograms. Dr. Harlow Shapley, who took Dr. Pickering's place as head of the Harvard observatory, told of once asking Cannon to locate a picture of the star SW Andromedae. She turned instantly to an assistant and asked, "Will you get Plate I 37311?"

In the years between 1915 and 1924, the *Henry Draper Catalog* was published in nine volumes. This series of books was the work that made Annie Cannon famous among astronomers. It contained a classification of all stars brighter than the ninth or 10th magnitude—a total of 225,300 stars. Astrophysicists still rely heavily on the *Henry Draper Catalog* in spite of all the advances that have been made in telescopic equipment since then.

Annie Cannon lived in a little house at the foot of Harvard's "observatory hill." She dubbed her home Star Cottage, and enjoyed entertaining visitors there. A powerful hearing aid helped her converse with her guests, who ranged from world-famous astronomers to young students.

Astronomy was one of the first sciences in which women were able to make a mark. Cannon wanted to see women astronomers taken seriously, so she cringed when she read about women who advertised themselves as astrologers and horoscope readers. That was mere superstition in Cannon's opinion, and she feared that it might contribute to the prejudice against women in astronomy. A member of the National Women's party, she worked to help get women the vote and rejoiced when the Nineteenth Amendment to the Constitution finally became law in 1920, ensuring this.

Harvard sent her to the Andes Mountains of Peru in 1922. There she spent six months working at Boyden Station, Harvard's South American observatory. This trip gave Cannon a chance to study and photograph the stars of the Southern Hemisphere, which are different from those she had been looking at all her life. While in Peru, she discovered a *nova* (a star that suddenly becomes brighter and then fades).

Cannon continued to catalog stars, adding many of the dimmer ones in the *Henry Draper Extension*, volumes of which were published in 1925 and 1949. During her lifetime she classified a total of more than 350,000 stars, more than anyone else had ever identified. She discovered 300 variable stars and five novae.

Annie Cannon received many honors and awards. In 1925, she became the first woman ever awarded an honorary doctorate by

Oxford University in England. She won the Draper Medal of the National Academy of Sciences in 1931 and the Ellen Richards Prize in 1932. Cannon used the money from the Richards Prize to set up an award specifically for women astronomers, eventually named the Annie Jump Cannon Prize. She was at one time the only female member of England's Royal Astronomical Society (although she was an honorary member because the society still barred women from regular membership). In 1938, Annie Cannon was named William Cranch Bond Astronomer at Harvard.

In 1925, Annie Cannon became the first woman ever to receive an honorary Doctor's degree from Oxford University.
(Photo courtesy Harvard College Observatory)

Described by friends as cheerful, charming, and enthusiastic, Annie Jump Cannon came to be known as "the dean of women astronomers." She was a legend at Harvard. Her painstaking cataloging of the stars made her a major influence on the development of the modern science of astronomy. She did not concern herself with theoretical questions about the underlying laws of nature, but was content to advance science's factual knowledge of the universe. A friend described her as "the happiest person I have ever known" (Emberlin, p. 27).

Throughout her life, Cannon loved to travel. She made many trips to Europe, often to attend professional meetings, but sometimes just to meet new people and visit new places.

Annie Cannon never got around to retiring. Through 1940 she was still working at the Harvard observatory at the age of 76. Early in 1941, heart disease finally forced her to stop. She died on Easter Sunday, 1941.

Cannon always drew comfort and strength from the stars. Knowing that light travels at a speed of 186,000 miles a second, she also knew how far away the stars are. Some of the starlight she studied was millions of years old. Yet the stars continued to appear to her eyes in their predictable patterns. To her they seemed to be patiently waiting for human beings to see them and enjoy their light.

In one of her last interviews she commented on the beginning of World War II: "In these days of great trouble and unrest, it is good to have something outside our own planet, something fine and distant and comforting to troubled minds. Let people look to the stars for comfort" (Emberlin, p. 27).

Chronology

December 11, 1863	Annie Jump Cannon is born in Dover, Delaware
1884	graduates from Wellesley College
1894	Becomes assistant to Sarah Whiting, Wellesley College
1895	starts as special student at Radcliffe College
1896	is hired as assistant at the Harvard observatory
1907	earns M.A., Wellesley
1910	Cannon's classification system wins general acceptance
1911	is named curator of photographs at Harvard observatory
1915–24	the *Henry Draper Catalog* is published
1922	Cannon works at Boyden Station in Peru; discovers a nova
1925	receives honorary doctorate, Oxford University; first volume of the *Henry Draper Extension* is published
1931	Cannon wins Draper Medal, National Academy of Sciences
1932	wins Ellen Richards Prize
1938	is named William Cranch Bond Astronomer, Harvard
April 13, 1941	dies of heart disease

Further Reading

Emberlin, Diane. *Science: Contributions of Women*. Minneapolis, MN: Dillon Press, 1977. This book for young readers contains a portrait of Annie Jump Cannon.

Gingerich, Owen. "Annie Jump Cannon." *Dictionary of Scientific Biography*. New York: Scribner, 1971, Vol. 3, pp. 49–50. Gives a brief sketch of Cannon's life and work.

McHenry, Robert, ed. *Liberty's Women*. Springfield, Massachusetts: G. & C. Merriam Co., 1980. Cannon is one of many American women whose achievements are listed in this book.

Ogilvie, Marilyn Bailey. *Women in Science*. Cambridge: MIT Press, 1986, pp. 51–52. Brief biographies of women scientists who lived and worked before the 20th century.

Yost, Edna. *American Women of Science*. New York: Lippincott, 1943. Yost's readable biography of Cannon is one chapter of this book.

Alice Hamilton
(1869–1970)

Alice Hamilton became one of the world's leading authorities on industrial medicine.
(Courtesy Library of Congress Photoduplication Service)

*T*hey called it *plumbism* (from *plumbum*, the Latin word for lead). The symptoms were shakiness, weight loss, headaches, vomiting, loss of muscle control, and sometimes paralysis. Some victims had convulsions, which people referred to as "lead fits." The disease was not caused by a virus or bacterium, but by lead poisoning. In the late 19th and early 20th centuries, it was a common cause of illness and death among American factory workers.

Many of the victims were immigrants who could barely speak English. Living in poverty in the slums of America's industrial cities, they were glad to get steady paychecks for their factory jobs, even if those jobs did expose them to lead. Those who became ill after a few years were easily replaced. Manufacturers and employees alike viewed lead poisoning as an unpleasant but necessary side effect, the price of progress. No one asked how many people developed the disease or what could be done to prevent it.

Then in 1908 the governor of Illinois appointed a committee to study the problem. A young Chicago physician named Alice Hamilton was asked to direct the investigation, which was scheduled to last for a year. The survey she conducted marked the beginning of a long career during which Hamilton became one of the world's leading experts on industrial medicine.

Alice Hamilton was born on February 27, 1869, in New York City, but she spent most of her early life in Fort Wayne, Indiana. Her grandfather, Allen Hamilton, had been one of the founders of Fort Wayne. Alice grew up on a family estate there, with three sisters, a brother, and 11 cousins. There were so many children on the grounds that they felt no need of outside friends. The girls did not go to school until each one was 17 years old; before that, they were tutored at home. It was a happy, privileged childhood.

The Hamilton cousins studied the subjects their parents considered important: languages, literature, history, a little math. They read many books on their own. And they played games based on their reading. As Alice later described her childhood: "In those days children invented their own games; grownups looked after health, studies, manners, and morals, but amusement was not their responsibility" (Hamilton, *Exploring the Dangerous Trades*, p. 25).

Montgomery Hamilton, Alice's father, was a gentle man who loved the classics and did not have a head for business. A partner in a wholesale grocery firm, he worked for years at an occupation he disliked and had no talent for. Alice's mother, Gertrude Pond Hamilton, encouraged her daughters to get an education and prepare themselves for careers. Gertrude Hamilton believed that personal freedom was necessary for a satisfying life; she did not want her girls to be totally dependent on husbands as most women were in those days.

The family attended the Presbyterian church, and Sundays were spent reading the Bible. But the children were never taught to believe unquestioningly whatever they were told. They were encouraged to think for themselves, to express their opinions, and to find evidence or logical reasons to support their statements. The moral code that they learned made them want to be of service, to make the world better.

When Alice was 17, she went to board at Miss Porter's School in Farmington, Vermont. The education she got there was not especially good; in fact, she said that "some of the teaching we received was the world's worst" (Hamilton, *Exploring the Dangerous Trades*, p. 35). Most classes required the students simply to memorize the textbook and recite it back word for word. There was no discussion. Since no courses were required, Alice took more of the subjects she already enjoyed, and avoided those she knew little about, such as math and science. School was easy for her, so she did not need to bother much about her studies.

She enjoyed her years in Vermont in spite of the questionable quality of the education she got there. She made lifelong friends at the school. Every day, each student was required to take a two-hour walk, and those walks gave Alice a love of the out-of-doors that was new to her. Miss Porter also emphasized values that stayed with most of the students: integrity, independence, respect for clear thinking, and a love of beauty.

Just before Alice went to Miss Porter's, her father's business had failed. Since the family finances had suddenly been reduced, she and her older sister Edith decided that they had better prepare themselves to earn their own livings and possibly even become able to help out at home. Edith decided to become a teacher, and she enrolled at Bryn Mawr, a women's college, to get her teaching degree. Alice chose medicine.

She had no background in science and was not even particularly interested in it. However, she thought that a career as a doctor would make her independent and allow her to be of use no matter where she went. Her family had trouble taking her ambition seriously. There were very few women doctors at the time, and Alice had never shown any particular aptitude for such work.

Realizing that she was not qualified for admission to medical school, Alice began by asking a high school teacher to tutor her in physics and chemistry. Then she took some courses at a small medical school in Fort Wayne. After several years of work she was accepted at the medical school of the University of Michigan.

The University of Michigan had admitted women for more than 20 years, but there were still few female students in the medical school. They would cluster together at the sides of the huge lecture halls and work together in the laboratories. Alice discovered that she did like science, especially lab work. She enjoyed learning to use microscopes and eventually decided to specialize in bacteriology (the study of various one-celled organisms, some of which cause disease) and pathology (the study of the nature, causes, and consequences of disease).

After finishing her course work, Alice interned first at the Northwestern Hospital for Women and Children in Minneapolis, Minnesota, and then at the New England Hospital for Women and Children just outside Boston. In Boston she worked at a dispensary (an office where people could get medicines and medical advice) in a poor area. It was her first exposure to real poverty. Many of the patients who came to the Pleasant Street Dispensary were recently arrived immigrants, trying to scratch out a living.

Faculty members back in Michigan had told Hamilton that, as a woman, she would have little chance of establishing a career as a pathologist without some advanced study. They had advised her to go to Europe and do graduate work there. Alice's older sister Edith had been given similar advice, so in 1894 the two sisters set out for Germany. Both of them found it hard to be taken seriously as female students. In fact, conditions there were even worse than they had been in the United States. Edith was made to sit on the platform, next to the professor, so that no one would have to sit beside her in the lecture hall. One professor thought that she should be placed behind a green curtain in the corner of the room. Alice ran into similar attitudes: "I had to accept the thinly veiled contempt of many of my teachers and fellow students because I was at once a woman and an American, therefore uneducated and incapable of real study" (Hamilton, *Exploring the Dangerous Trades*, p. 47).

In spite of these problems, Alice was able to do some useful laboratory research. She enjoyed the international scientific meetings she was able to attend, and the concerts, and some of the people she met in Germany. But in addition to the negative attitude toward women she saw there, she was distressed by German anti-Semitism and militarism.

The Hamilton sisters returned home in the fall of 1896. Edith got a job as headmistress of the Bryn Mawr School in Baltimore. Unable to find a job herself, Alice joined her sister in Baltimore to study pathological anatomy at Johns Hopkins University.

In the summer of 1897, Alice Hamilton was invited to teach pathology at the Women's Medical School of Northwestern University just north of Chicago, Illinois. The prospect of moving to the area made her decide to try to get a room at Hull House. There was no space available when she first arrived, but Hamilton was soon able to move into the famous settlement house.

Hull House had been founded by Jane Addams in 1889. Alice Hamilton had heard Addams speak at the Methodist Church in Fort Wayne several years earlier and had been interested in the project ever since. The idea behind the settlement house movement was that trained and dedicated people would live together in a poor neighborhood and donate their services to the people of the area. They received no salaries for this, so they all worked at other jobs in addition to their volunteer services.

Hamilton opened a well-baby clinic in the basement. She had eight little bathtubs there, and much of her work had to do with getting the children clean and encouraging mothers to keep them clean. Immigrants from warm climates were afraid of the midwestern winters, and sometimes brought their children sewn into winter clothes. Hamilton also taught nutrition and gave medical advice to the young mothers.

She developed a great sympathy and respect for these poor women. They faced terrible choices: should I leave my child alone while I work as a scrubwoman or put the child in an orphanage? Should I work in a factory for $8 a week or earn more as a prostitute? How can I leave my drunken, abusive husband when his paycheck is the only income I have to feed my children?

Her work at Hull House made Hamilton aware of the injustices in American life. She had been raised to believe in equal opportunity for all, but she quickly saw that opportunities for the slum children of Chicago were not the same as those she had enjoyed. For the rest of her life, she fought against economic and social injustice.

Hamilton taught pathology to the female medical students at Northwestern University for five years. Then, when Northwestern decided to combine the men's and women's medical schools, she went to work at the Memorial Institute for Infectious Diseases, doing research in bacteriology.

During these years, Hamilton fought against the spread of cocaine. Residents of Hull House discovered that many school dropouts were sniffing "happy dust," which could easily be bought at neighborhood drugstores. The laws of the time did little to prevent sale and use of cocaine and other drugs. Hamilton personally visited many drugstore owners and tried to persuade them not to sell the addictive powder to children.

She also provided birth control information to poor women. Every child meant another mouth to feed, and the families in the area often had more children than they could care for. Hamilton once heard an Italian immigrant telling about how she had thrown herself down the cellar stairs in an attempt to end a pregnancy.

Among the men in the Hull House neighborhood, one of the most common health problems was lead poisoning. Many of them worked in factories where lead was used, and after a few years they would begin to show the symptoms of the disease. Hamilton read a book by an English doctor, Sir Thomas Oliver, called *The Dangerous Trades*. She learned that steps were being taken overseas to protect workers, but it seemed that almost no one was concerned about similar problems in the United states. Manufacturers claimed that factories in the United States were more advanced than those in Europe and that illnesses that did occur were due to the carelessness and ignorance of the immigrant workers.

In 1909 Hamilton went to Europe to attend the International Congress on Occupational Accidents and Diseases held that year in Belgium. At the meeting she became acquainted with Charles O'Neill, commissioner of labor in the U.S. Commerce Department. Impressed with her knowledge and concern, he asked Hamilton to investigate the situation in the United States and report her findings. She agreed to work on this without legal authority and without a salary. After the meeting, she toured factories that had taken safety measures to protect workers from lead poisoning. In England she saw a plant with 90 employees that had not had a case of lead poisoning in five years.

Back in Illinois, Hamilton discussed her concern with others who were aware of the hazards of lead poisoning. In 1910 a sociologist named Charles Henderson persuaded the governor to appoint an Occupational Disease Commission to look into the matter. Illinois was the first state to conduct such an investigation. Alice Hamilton was one of five doctors appointed to the commission, and she was selected to head the survey that was to be done.

She found a grim situation in the factories of Illinois. No safety inspection was ever done by any outside body. When an employee was injured or became ill on the job, he was taken to a company hospital and treated by company doctors. Often he was not even allowed to communicate with his family. Medical records were sketchy or nonexistent. Hamilton and her assistants had to go through records in which patients were identified only as "Joe" or "Karl." Workers could sue their employers, but it was almost impossible for them to win even if they could afford to pay lawyers. The law said that a person knowingly took a risk when going to work in an industrial job, and employers could not be held responsible in most cases.

Employers did not want to see health problems as their fault. They insisted that the symptoms of lead poisoning were caused by alcoholism or that the workers refused to wash their hands after exposure to lead. Hamilton discovered that the most serious illnesses resulted from breathing lead dust in the workplace.

Hamilton and her assistants worked long hours visiting plants, interviewing diseased workers and their families, and going through medical records. Eventually they were able to document 22 cases of *plumbism*, or lead poisoning, caused by industrial exposure. They were sure that many more existed. In addition to lead, they investigated the dangers of arsenic, brass, carbon monoxide, cyanide, and turpentine. All these substances were suspected of causing health problems, and all were widely used in manufacturing. Hamilton visited factories making a wide variety of products: coffins, pottery, bathtubs, and even cigars (the "tin foil" in which they were wrapped was really lead). The commission's findings were published in a report called *A Survey of Occupational Diseases*.

In 1911, as a result of the survey report, Illinois passed a law providing for financial compensation for victims of industrial hazards. Thus the employers had to get insurance to cover the cost of compensation. Insurance companies insisted that the factories take safety measures, and so the precautions that already existed overseas came into use in the United States. By the late 1930s all the states had enacted laws modeled after Illinois'.

After 1911, Alice Hamilton went on to conduct a national survey, as she had promised to do. Once again, she began her work with the dangers of lead poisoning, since that seemed to be one of the worst problems in Illinois. She visited lead smelting plants all over the United States, as well as other manufacturers that used lead. Among these were paint makers, many of whom thought that good paint could not be made without lead. Residents of houses painted with these old lead paints are still having health problems today because of it.

During the First World War, Hamilton inspected plants making explosives. These were secret, so she had difficulty even locating them. Once in a train station in New Jersey she saw two workmen whose clothes were covered with yellow stains. They told her they worked in a plant making *picric*, a poisonous yellow substance used in explosives. She managed to locate the factory but had to run away from the fumes. There was no protection whatsoever for the employees. The attitude of the managers was that if they died, it was simply part of the war effort.

By 1919, Alice Hamilton was the leading American authority on lead poisoning, and one of the few specialists on industrial diseases in the world. Harvard University wanted to offer course work in that area, so they invited Hamilton to join their faculty as an assistant professor. She accepted the position on the condition that it be half time only, so that she could continue the federal survey. Hamilton then became the first woman faculty member at Harvard University. She was not allowed to enter the all-male Harvard Club or even to march at Commencement, but the faculty at one of America's most prestigious universities would never again be closed to women.

As the survey continued, Hamilton developed into a skilled negotiator. She was never satisfied with merely pointing out abuses; she wanted to convince employers to correct them. Only a few of the employers she encountered were truly heartless. Most were willing to make changes once she had convinced them that the problems were real. Frank Hammar of Hammar Brothers White Lead company got the National Lead Institute to sponsor some of Hamilton's research at Harvard. Edward Cornish, president of the National Lead Company, installed all the safety measures Hamilton suggested at all his plants and hired doctors to monitor the results. Walter Kohler made all his enameling plants dust-free after Hamilton pointed out the dangers of the lead dust. General Electric hired her as a consultant from 1923 to 1933.

In 1925, Hamilton published the first American textbook on the subject of industrial diseases, *Industrial Poisons in the United States*. This book allowed Hamilton to share what she had learned with a much wider audience, and it made her one of the two leading authorities in the world.

In 1935, having reached the usual retirement age of 65, Hamilton was forced to retire from Harvard. Still energetic, she looked for other opportunities to use her knowledge and experience. Jane Addams died the same year, and Hamilton was invited to take over the leadership at Hull House, but she declined. Instead, she became a consultant for the Division of Labor Standards of the

U.S. Department of Labor. In this position she continued to study industrial hazards and did a great deal of testifying before congressional committees and at hearings. Hamilton also served on the health committee of the League of Nations. She wrote her autobiography, *Exploring the Dangerous Trades*, published in 1943, and revised her textbook for a new edition published in 1949. From 1944 to 1949 she served as national president of the Consumers' League.

Hamilton had opposed the Equal Rights Amendment when it was first proposed in the 1920s because she thought it would take

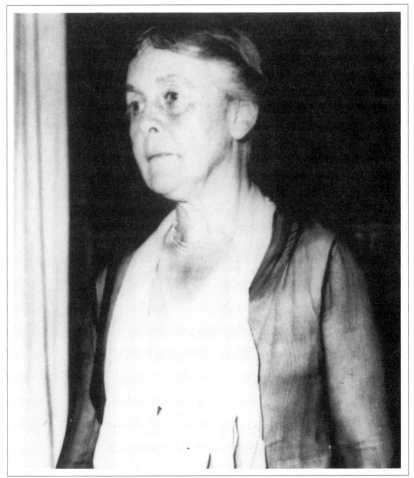

Alice Hamilton in 1933.
(Photo courtesy UPI/Bettmann)

away needed legal protections for poor women. However, in 1952 she changed her mind and withdrew her opposition to the amendment. She liked to keep up with current issues, even in old age. Hamilton wrote many letters to editors and congressmen protesting the strong anticommunist feeling that ran U.S. foreign policy and threatened civil liberties in America. She was an early supporter of U.S. recognition of the People's Republic of China. In 1963, at 94, she signed an open letter calling for the withdrawal of American troops from Vietnam.

Alice Hamilton was still living in her own home when she died of a stroke at the age of 101 on September 22, 1970.

Her fame as the founder of the science of industrial medicine in the United States and as the first woman professor at Harvard meant little to Hamilton. At the age of 88, looking back on her already long life, she said: "For me the satisfaction is that things are better now, and I had some part in it" (*Notable American Women*, p. 306).

Due largely to the work of Alice Hamilton, every state has laws to protect employees from injury and disease caused by their jobs. A large division of the U.S. Public Health Service oversees industrial hazards nationally. Workers are no longer willing to submit meekly to dangerous conditions at their jobs, and employers can get reliable information on plant safety.

Alice Hamilton's field work provided a great deal of knowledge about on-the-job health hazards and how to prevent them. During her long career, she identified and publicized new industrial poisons as they came on the market. Her success made it easier for women to be taken seriously as scientists and medical experts.

Those who knew her personally admired her accomplishments but also enjoyed her company. She was easy to be with, a dynamo at work and a caring, lively, stimulating person in social groups. Hamilton never took herself so seriously that she lost interest in others and in the world around her.

During most of Alice Hamilton's lifetime, it was seen as not only unusual but downright radical for a woman to challenge established authority as she did. She succeeded because she knew what she was talking about and because she was not afraid to take unpopular stands once she had the facts. Her willingness to risk being seen as a troublemaker allowed her to cause lasting changes in American life; because of her work, the dangerous trades would never be as dangerous again.

Chronology

February 27, 1869	Alice Hamilton is born
1886	Hamilton enters Miss Porter's school
1893–94	earns M.D. degree, University of Michigan; does internships
1896	does research and studies at Johns Hopkins University
1897	joins faculty of Women's Medical School, Northwestern University
1902	is appointed bacteriologist, Memorial Institute for Infectious Diseases; investigates typhoid epidemic
1908	is appointed to the Illinois Commission on Occupational Diseases
1910	publishes *Survey of Occupational Diseases*
1911	is appointed special investigator, U.S. Bureau of Labor; begins federal survey
1919	is named professor of industrial medicine, Harvard University
1923–33	works as medical consultant, General Electric
1925	publishes *Industrial Poisons in the United States*, first text on that subject
1935	retires from Harvard; becomes consultant for the Division of Labor Standards, Department of Labor
1943	publishes autobiography, *Exploring the Dangerous Trades*
1944–49	serves as president, National Consumer's League
Sept. 22, 1970	dies at age of 101

Further Reading

Boynick, David King. *Women Who Led the Way: Eight Pioneers For Equal Rights*. New York: Crowell, 1972. Profiles of eight determined individuals who made a difference, including Alice Hamilton.

Brin, Ruth. *Contributions of Women: Social Reform*. Minneapolis, MN: Dillon Press, 1977. A profile of Hamilton is included in this collection of brief biographies of women who brought about social change.

Grant, Madeline. *Alice Hamilton: Pioneer Doctor in Industrial Medicine*. Abelard-Schuman, 1967. Focuses on Hamilton's long professional career and her influence in bringing social reform.

Hamilton, Alice. *Exploring the Dangerous Trades*. Boston: Little, Brown, 1943. Hamilton's autobiography gives an interesting, well-written account of her unusual childhood and her life at Hull House as well as a detailed description of her work.

Notable American Women, Modern period, "Alice Hamilton". Cambridge: Harvard University Press, 1980, pp. 303–306. Brief overview of Hamilton's life and the importance of her work as a "pioneer in industrial toxicology."

Marks, Geoffrey, and Beatty, William K. *Women in White*. New York: Scribner, 1972. History of women in medicine since ancient times. Includes a discussion of Alice Hamilton.

Schacher, Susan. *Hypatia's Sisters: Biographies of Women Scientists, Past and Present*. Feminists Northwest, 1976. Hamilton is included in this collection of brief biographies.

Edith Quimby
(1891–1982)

Edith Quimby was a pioneering researcher in
radiation physics.
(Photo courtesy National Archives)

*R*adiation physics is a 20th-century science, and its development
helped to shape the history of the 20th century. From its earliest
beginnings, women scientists have played a major role in creating
and expanding this new field of knowledge. It was Marie Curie,
with her husband Pierre, who in 1898 discovered and isolated a
previously unknown substance that gave off powerful rays that
came to be called *radioactive*. Marie Curie later founded the
Radium Institute in Paris, where she and her daughter, Irene

Curie, began studies on the use of radiation in treating disease. Both Marie and Irene Curie won the Nobel Prize. So did an American woman, Rosalyn Yalow, whose work will be described later in this book. And Yalow began her career as an assistant in the laboratory of Edith Quimby.

Quimby was born Edith Hinkley on July 10, 1891, in Rockford, Illinois. Her father, Arthur S. Hinkley, had been trained as an architect but also did some farming. He could not seem to settle anywhere permanently. At various times during Edith's childhood the family lived in Illinois, Alabama, California, and Idaho. Edith and her sister and brother learned how to adjust to new neighborhoods and new schools during these years.

Always a good student, Edith showed special aptitude for science. A high school teacher in Boise, Idaho, encouraged her to go on to college and perhaps prepare for a career as a science teacher. In 1908, Edith enrolled at Whitman College in Walla Walla, Washington. Whitman, one of the oldest colleges in the Pacific Northwest, welcomed female students at a time when many of the larger universities were still closed to women. Encouraged by Professor Brown, her physics. teacher, Edith took a double major in mathematics and physics.

After graduation in 1912, she took a job as a science teacher at a high school in Nyssa, Oregon. Although she enjoyed teaching, Edith was not satisfied with the thought of spending the rest of her life going through the same material in high school physics. She wanted to know more, and possibly do more, than that.

In 1914, Edith Hinkley was awarded a fellowship to do graduate work in physics at the University of California. There she met and married a fellow student, Shirley L. Quimby. Edith Quimby received her master's degree in physics in 1916. She and her new husband then moved to Antioch, California, where he had been hired to teach high school science. Two years later, the United States entered the First World War. Shirley Quimby enlisted in the navy, and while he was away Edith filled his teaching post.

The Quimbys moved from California to New York City in 1919, where Shirley Quimby had a new job as an instructor in physics at Columbia University. While holding this position he would also do more graduate work toward a Ph.D. in physics.

Edith also wanted to work, and she began looking for jobs that would allow her to do some research in physics. Her husband heard that Dr. Gioacchino Failla, chief physicist at the Memorial Hospital for Cancer and Allied Diseases in New York City, needed an assistant. Edith applied for the job. Although it was most unusual for a woman to seek such a position in those days, Dr. Failla was so impressed with Edith Quimby that he hired her.

This was the beginning of a partnership that lasted more than 30 years. At first, Quimby was clearly an assistant, following Dr. Failla's orders rather than working on her own. But as time went on, she proved herself to be an outstanding scientist in her own right. The two became collaborators. At that time, Edith Quimby became the only woman in America who was engaged in medical physics research. She also became one of the founders of the new science of radiation physics.

Substances such as radium are called radioactive because they give off penetrating rays. A radioactive nucleus is unstable; that is, it can't hold itself together. At times it will send out a small particle of itself. Streams of these tiny particles are always being sent forth from a radioactive substance.

These rays can penetrate solid substances such as human skin. One of the first practical applications of radioactivity was the use of X rays for diagnosis. Until the development of X rays, doctors either had to guess what was going on inside a patient's body or cut the body open to find out. Now, using X rays, they could take pictures of conditions that could not be seen from outside.

Scientists also discovered that radioactive rays can be used to kill cancer cells while leaving healthy cells alone. This is because cancer cells divide faster than normal cells. When exposed to radiation, the cancer cells react quickly. A dose of radiation too small to hurt healthy cells can therefore kill the cancer cells.

When Quimby and Failla began their work, some American doctors were beginning to experiment with radiation treatment of cancerous tumors. The problem was that no one knew how to calculate the proper dosage. Too much radiation, and the treatment could be worse than the disease. Too little, and it was ineffective. People of different ages and sizes needed different dosages. Physicians tried to determine the proper amounts of radiation by trial and error, but it was a risky business. There were other problems in treating cancer with radiation. Doctors and nurses had to be able to administer the rays only to the diseased parts of the patients' bodies. They had to be able to do this without injuring themselves in the process.

Scientists who worked to increase knowledge in this area called their field *radiology* (the study of radiant energy for medical use). Gioacchino Failla and Edith Quimby were two of the first physicists to conduct research in radiology.

In the beginning, they worked only with radium, the radioactive substance that Marie Curie had isolated. The first radium produced in the United States had become available for the first time in 1913, through a process so difficult and expensive that the first gram sold for $120,000. Quimby and Failla worked in one of the few laboratories in the country that was able to invest enough money in radium and equipment to make research possible.

One of Edith Quimby's main jobs was to measure radioactive rays so as to determine exactly how much radiation came out of a specific amount of radium, how much stayed on the skin, and how much penetrated through the skin. At the time, radiation was measured in *roentgens*, units of measurement named for Wilhelm Roentgen, a pioneering German physicist. Quimby used instruments that measured the amount of electricity generated by any given amount of radioactive material. These measurements were carefully recorded so that the guesswork could be taken out of radiation therapy.

Quimby and Failla also used laboratory animals to study the effects of radiation on living tissue. They were able to observe the effects of radioactive rays on tumors in these animals, and to draw conclusions about necessary dosages for human patients. Because their laboratory was located in a fine hospital, they could also observe the treatment of human cancer patients and see the results of various dosages.

Their knowledge grew slowly and steadily. Physicians everywhere were eager for more guidance in the use of radiation therapy, so it was important to tell them about the results of the laboratory work. Between 1920 and 1940, Edith Quimby published 50 technical articles explaining what she and Failla had learned. Doctors were able to use this information to calculate the exact dosage needed to treat each cancer patient.

Although she had started out as an assistant to Dr. Failla, Edith Quimby quickly became an equal partner. She was officially promoted from assistant to associate physicist in 1932.

In 1940, Edith Quimby was awarded the Janeway Medal by the American Radiation Society. She was the first woman ever to receive this award. She also received an honorary doctorate from her alma mater, Whitman College. 1941 brought her another honor, the Gold Medal of the Radiological Society of North America.

As radiation therapy became more commonly used and more complicated, medical schools needed help in teaching physicians how to use it. Edith Quimby was appointed assistant professor of radiology at the Cornell University Medical School in 1941. By this time, radiology had become a specialty in medicine, and Quimby knew more about it than almost anyone else did.

In 1941, the United States entered World War II. Ever since the fighting had begun in Europe, American scientists had been talking about how they might help the war effort if America did become involved. The most promising area of work was in radiation physics. Researchers were close to splitting the atom (the smallest unit of an element that has all of that element's properties). This would release enormous amounts of energy. They believed that splitting the atom might make it possible to create an atomic bomb.

Preliminary work along these lines had begun at Columbia University in 1939. Professor John R. Dunning and other faculty members had built a small *cyclotron* (an apparatus used in nuclear experiments) in the basement of the physics building at Columbia. A large area on the seventh floor was also being used for investigations of the possible war uses of nuclear energy. All of this was top secret, but rumors did circulate about the existence of a mysterious scientific effort called the Manhattan Project.

In 1942, both Dr. Failla and Edith Quimby joined the faculty at Columbia University. From that time until the end of the war, Quimby worked half-time for the Manhattan Project. She was not one of the leading figures in the development of the atomic bomb, but like most other prominent physicists of the time, she contributed to the work on it. After the war she continued to work for the Atomic Energy Commission, which was then trying to develop peaceful uses of atomic energy.

At Columbia, Edith Quimby became a teacher again. She created a course in the new science of radiation physics that became an important part of the medical education physicians received there. Once again as at Cornell, Quimby taught future doctors how to use radiation safely in the treatment of disease.

During the late 1940s, Quimby helped to make possible the synthetic production of radioactive sodium. This laboratory-made substance could then be used in medical research. As more and more uses for radioactivity became known, there was also a need for more concern about safety. Quimby had long been aware of the hazards of working with radioactive materials. She had begun publishing warnings of the dangers of overexposure in the 1920s. After World War II she used her laboratory to investigate safety measures. In 1957 she won a medal from the American Cancer Society in recognition of her work.

Quimby won the Katharine Berkan Judd Award on March 12, 1962.
(Photo courtesy UPI/Bettmann)

People paid attention to Edith Quimby when she expressed her opinions or gave advice. She was tall, with piercing gray eyes and an air of self-confidence. Quimby kept herself well informed on events outside the laboratory. An active member of the League of Women Voters, she maintained a strong interest in politics.

Edith Quimby moved up quickly in the ranks of the Columbia University faculty, although she was one of the few female teachers at the College of Physicians and Surgeons and also one of very few faculty members who were not physicians. Her outstanding record as a teacher and researcher was recognized in 1954 when she was named a full professor. In 1960, when she was ready to retire, Columbia appointed her professor emeritus.

Another honor was the Katharine Berkan Judd Award, which is given to a scientist who "shall have made the greatest advancement to the discovery of a cure for cancer." Quimby received this award on March 12, 1962, from Alfred P. Sloan, Jr., founder of the Sloan-Kettering Institute for Cancer Research.

Quimby had been one of the founding members of the American Association of Physicists in Medicine (AAPM). In 1978 that organization gave her the William D. Coolidge Award, which recognizes distinguished careers and important contributions to medical physics. The award honored her as a pioneer in her field.

Continuing to work as long as she was able, Dr. Quimby served on the Atomic Energy Commission's Committee for the Control and Distribution of Radioactive Isotopes and the National Committee for Radiation Protection. She was also an examiner for the American Board of Radiology.

Edith Quimby died on October 11, 1982, at the age of 91. The many obituaries that appeared at the time recognized her as one of the founders of the science of radiation physics. They noted her importance as the teacher of more than a thousand physicians who used radiology in their work. They pointed out her important contributions to scientists' knowledge of proper dosages in radiation treatments. They referred to the more than 75 articles she had published.

Above all, these obituaries recognized Dr. Edith Quimby as one of the first physicists to see the possibilities in the new area of nuclear medicine. In the years since her pioneering work began, hundreds of thousands of people have benefited from it. Few of the patients whose cancerous tumors have been treated with radiation therapy ever heard of Edith Quimby. But there is a sense in which she lives on in every person who recovers health because of a form of treatment she helped to make possible.

Chronology

July 10, 1891	Edith Hinkley is born in Rockford, Illinois
1912	earns B.S. degree, Whitman College
1914	does graduate studies, University of California
1915	marries Shirley L. Quimby
1916	earns M.A. degree, University of California
1919	becomes assistant to Dr. Gioacchino Failla, New York City Memorial Hospital for Cancer and Allied Diseases
1919–1940	experiments with radiation doses; publishes results
1932	promoted to associate physicist
1941	is awarded Janeway Medal, American Radium Society; receives honorary doctorate, Whitman College; appointed assistant professor, Cornell University Medical School
1942	is hired by the College of Physicians and Surgeons, Columbia University; begins work on the Manhattan Project
1943	named associate professor of radiology, College of Physicians and Surgeons, Columbia University
1954	appointed full professor, Columbia University; wins Medal of the American Cancer Society
1960	retires; named professor emeritus
1962	receives Katharine Berkan Judd Award
1978	receives Coolidge Award, American Association of Physicists in Medicine
October 11, 1982	dies at age 91

Further Reading

"Coolidge Award to Edith Quimby." *Physics Today*, January, 1978, p. 89. Brief article recognizes Quimby's lifetime achievements.

Current Biography Yearbook 1949, pp. 492–93. Biographical sketch provides information on Quimby's life up to 1949.

Current Biography, March, 1983, p. 45. Obituary of Edith Quimby.

Emberlin, Diane. *Contributions of Women: Science*. Minneapolis, MN: Dillon Press, 1977, pp. 153–54. This book provides a one-page profile of Edith Quimby.

The New York Times, October 13, 1982, p. A-28 (obituary). Quimby's most significant achievements are described, along with the major events in her life.

Noble, Iris, *Contemporary Women Scientists of America*. New York: Julian Messner, 1979, pp. 14–15. This young adult book includes a readable and helpful sketch of Quimby's work.

Yost, Edna. *Women of Modern Science*. New York: Dodd, Mead, 1960. One chapter of this young adult book is devoted to Edith Quimby. Yost based it on interviews with Quimby.

Gerty Cori
(1896–1957)

Gerty Cori, biochemist at Washington University in St. Louis, won the Nobel Prize in 1947.
(Photo courtesy Washington University in St. Louis)

---

*W*hen feeling tired, many people grab a candy bar for a quick burst of energy. Most people know that sugar and other *carbohydrates* are used by the body as fuel that allows them to be active and alert—but how does this happen? And why does the process go wrong in some people? Gerty Cori spent most of her life seeking answers to these questions. Because of the work she did alone and with her husband, Carl F. Cori, scientists could better understand how the human body changes food into energy, and how to help when this natural system does not function as it should.

Gerty Radnitz was born August 15, 1896, in Prague, Austria-Hungary (now Czechoslovakia), the oldest daughter of Otto and Martha Radnitz.

She did not go to school until she was 10 years old but was tutored at home. At 10 she entered a private girls' school. Some time during the next few years, she decided that she wanted to study medicine. This interest may have been encouraged by an uncle who was a physician. Gerty's education had been weak in science and math, but she studied hard and by the age of 16 was ready to enter college and begin her medical studies.

She enrolled at the German University of Prague in the fall of 1914. This was a frightening time in Europe. All summer, Austria-Hungary had been preparing for war; European countries were lining up in two opposing camps. Gerty probably watched Kaiser Wilhelm's German troops marching with the Austrians through the streets of Prague. On the other side were the French, Russians, and British. (The United States was neutral until 1918.) By September, all Europe was being torn apart by the brutal conflict.

But there were no battles being fought in Prague, and Gerty Radnitz dove into her classes enthusiastically. An attractive young woman with thick, red-brown hair, she must have stood out in a school where most of the students were men. One young man who noticed her was Carl Cori. They met in anatomy class and quickly learned that they had much in common: a passion for science, a desire to go into research, a love of the out-of-doors, and an interest in tennis and other sports.

They decided to do a research project together. The topic was the immune bodies of the blood. When the lab work was done, they wrote a paper reporting the results. This was the beginning of a remarkable partnership that would last for the rest of Gerty's life.

It took six years for Gerty and Carl to finish college and earn their medical degrees. By the time they graduated, in 1920, the war had ended, but conditions in Europe were still bad. The young couple married soon after graduation, and they began to talk about coming to America.

Carl got a teaching job at the University of Graz, and an assistantship in the medical clinic at the University of Vienna. Gerty found a position as an assistant at the Karolinen Children's Hospital in Vienna. This was a pattern that would continue through most of their lives. Although Gerty was just as good a student as Carl and equally skilled as a researcher, and although whenever possible they did their work together, Carl Cori always got better jobs and more recognition than his wife. He would find a post somewhere and then she would follow along and get a lesser position. The Coris never competed with each other or felt like rivals, but they had a hard time getting equal treatment in the academic and scientific communities.

After two years in Vienna, Carl Cori was hired as a *pathologist* (one who studies the nature, causes, and consequences of disease) by the New York State Institute for the Study of Malignant Diseases, later known as Roswell Park Memorial Institute, in Buffalo. He came alone. A few months later, the institute was persuaded to offer Gerty a job as an assistant pathologist, and she, too, came to America.

During that summer of 1922, a Canadian doctor named Frederick Banting isolated the hormone *insulin* and began using it to treat diabetes. Until then, diabetics had been doomed to live short, miserable lives. Their bodies could not change carbohydrates such as sugar into energy. Instead, the sugars from their food stayed in the bloodstream, causing them to suffer from terrible thirst and hunger, weight loss, lack of energy, and eventually, coma and death. But when they got regular injections of insulin, they could live normal lives.

Hormones are substances that are manufactured in one part of the body and travel to another, stimulating that other part to do its job in keeping the body functioning. Banting showed that insulin, which is made in the pancreas, somehow tells the body to burn carbohydrates, turning them into energy. The pancreas of a diabetic does not produce enough insulin to use up all the carbohydrates that are taken in as food.

Banting's discovery made a treatment for diabetes possible. However, scientists still did not understand just how carbohydrates are converted into energy or how much insulin is needed to accomplish the conversion. Doctors had to experiment with diets and insulin shots, trying to find the best treatment for each individual patient. More knowledge was needed about this whole process.

Carl and Gerty Cori decided to work on this research at the institute. They already knew that carbohydrates turn into *glucose*, a sugar, during digestion and that the glucose is absorbed into the blood, where it is converted into energy. They knew that some leftover glucose, like the ashes after a wood fire, remained and became *glycogen*, a form of starch. The glycogen can then be stored in the liver and muscles and released when the blood sugar gets low. It is then changed back into glucose.

This process became the focus of the Coris' work. They stayed in Buffalo for nine years, doing research together for most of that time. It was not always easy. Once, Gerty was told that she would be fired if she did not stop working with Carl. The Coris refused to stop, and fearful that they might lose both scientists, the supervisors finally backed down. Later, Carl went to be interviewed for a job at another university. He was offered the job on the condition that only he would be hired. Gerty, who had come along for the interview, was told that she was "standing in the way of her husband's career" and that it was "un-American for a man to work with his wife" (Parascandola, p. 166). Carl did not accept that job offer.

In 1928, Carl and Gerty Cori became naturalized United States citizens. They developed a great love of their adopted country, especially in view of the ominous events back in Germany and Austria. The rise of Hitler destroyed any thoughts they might have had about returning "home." Later in her life, Gerty Cori told an interviewer: "I believe that the benefits of two civilizations, followed by the freedom and opportunities of this country, have been essential to whatever contributions I have been able to make to science" (Opfell, p. 192).

The Coris continued to work in Buffalo. They kept white rats in their laboratory and fed them sugar. Some were also given insulin. By studying these laboratory animals over a period of time, they began to learn more about the chemical changes that take place as the body uses food. In the late 1920s they published a series of papers presenting their findings.

In 1931, Carl Cori was offered a position as professor of biochemistry and pharmacology at Washington University in St. Louis, Missouri. This time provisions were made so that Gerty could continue to work with him. She was hired as a research assistant in pharmacology and so was able to use the same laboratory and to continue to explore the mysteries of *metabolism* (the processes by which human bodies are able to maintain life) with her husband.

The Coris took the muscles from frogs' legs, cut them into small pieces, and soaked them in distilled water. After three soakings, the glucose had been washed away, but the glycogen stored in the muscles remained. Using various chemicals, they extracted from this glycogen a substance that had never been studied before. It was a form of glucose, but it was different from the glucose usually found in the blood. They called it *glucose-1-phosphate* (glucose must combine with phosphate in order to be used by the body). Later, other scientists named it *Cori-ester*. The Coris also identified two new *enzymes* (proteins that cause chemical changes in the blood). This work allowed the Coris to describe exactly how the body converts carbohydrates into energy. The process goes on in a continuing cycle, which came to be known as the *Cori cycle*. They also demonstrated for the first time that an enzyme defect can cause inheritable disease in humans.

None of this was discovered quickly or easily. It took most of the 1930s and 1940s for Carl and Gerty Cori to reach their most important conclusions. Such laboratory work is slow and tedious, and one of the reasons they insisted on working together was that the two of them could accomplish more than either one could have done alone. An article in the *New York Post* described their cooperative method this way: " . . . it is hard to tell where the work of one leaves off and that of the other begins. They talk over their problems together, decide what is to be done, and then parcel the tasks out between them, checking and correlating with each other all the way" (quoted in Opfell, p. 189).

For many years, Gerty Cori and her husband, Carl, did research together.
(Photo courtesy Washington University in St. Louis)

Their first and only child, Carl Thomas, was born in 1936. Gerty was 40 years old at the time. Carl Thomas eventually grew up to earn his own Ph.D. and become a research biochemist.

In 1946, Carl Cori won the Lasker Basic Medical Research Award, a gold statuette of the Winged Victory of Samothrace. Although Gerty had contributed to every step of the research for which he was honored, she did not share in this award. No woman had ever won it, and it was not until 30 years later, when Rosalyn Yalow received the Lasker Award, that the committee choosing the recipient was ready to recognize a woman's achievements in medical research.

However, 1947 brought advancement and recognition to both Coris. Carl was named head of the department of biochemistry at Washington University, and Gerty was made a full professor in the same department.

That summer, while climbing Snow Mass Peak in Colorado, Gerty began to notice the first symptoms of the disease that was to take her life. When she got home, doctors told her she had *myelofibrosis*, a rare cancer of the bone marrow that usually proves fatal. They could not tell her how long she might live, but she knew that she and Carl would have to make the most of the time they had left.

In November of the same year, 1947, there was good news. Their research on enzymes had won the Nobel Prize in Physiology or Medicine. The prize recognized the importance of their description of the chemical reaction by which glycogen is used in the human body. This time, Gerty would share the prize with her husband and with an Argentinian doctor named Bernardo Houssay, who had been doing similar work. Gerty Cori was the first American woman to win a Nobel Prize in the sciences. The Coris flew to Stockholm, Sweden, to accept their prize. Both of them spoke at the official ceremony, though only Carl was invited to make a speech at the evening banquet.

Gerty Cori lived for 10 more years and kept on working for most of that time. The symptoms of her disease grew steadily worse, but she courageously went on doing what she could. Because myelofibrosis causes anemia, she had to have frequent blood transfusions. Growing gradually weaker, she was forced to give up the outdoor exercise that had been so much a part of her life. Still she kept working in the laboratory and teaching. She also liked to befriend international students who were often lonely in a strange country, as she had once been.

Carl and Gerty Cori did not always work together. During her last years, Gerty did much research on her own, with the help of graduate students. She studied the molecular structure of glycogen (its physical makeup), creating a method for doing this and for recording the results. Her findings helped her to identify several types of disease related to the storage of glycogen. She made useful contributions to the study of diabetes in children.

In 1950, President Harry S. Truman appointed Gerty Cori to the Board of Directors of the National Science Foundation, a post she kept until her death.

The lab shared by Carl and Gerty Cori had become a center for research on metabolism by this time. Other scientists were able to build on what the Coris had learned, adding to their knowledge of health, disease, and human life. Through a combination of genius and hard work, this couple paved the way for many advances in the treatment of illnesses such as diabetes. Arne Tiselius, vice president of the Nobel Foundation, had said that the Coris helped people to understand "the intricate patterns of chemical reactions in the living cells, where everything appears to depend on everything else" (Opfell, p. 191).

Gerty Cori's most important personal values were courage, kindness, and honesty. Near the end of her life she said that honesty had been most important to her when she'd been younger, but that with the years she came to value kindness even more.

On October 26, 1957, Gerty Cori died at the age of 61. A recording of a radio program she had appeared on was played at the memorial service. Family and friends who had gathered to remember Gerty heard her own voice speaking about her work: "For a research worker the unforgotten moments of life are those rare ones, which come after years of plodding work, when the veil over nature's secret seems suddenly to lift and when what was dark and chaotic appears in a clear and beautiful light pattern." For her, science had almost been an art form. She told the mourners: "I believe that in art and science are the glories of the human mind. I see no conflict between them" (Parascandola, p. 167).

Chronology

▬▬▬▬▬

August 15, 1896   Gerty Radnitz is born in Prague, Austria-Hungary (now Czechoslovakia)

1920   earns medical degree, German University of Prague; marries Carl Cori; begins work at Karolinen Children's Hospital, Vienna

1922   comes to United States to join staff of New York State Institute for the Study of Malignant Diseases

1928   becomes naturalized U.S. citizen

1931   moves to Washington University, St. Louis, Missouri

1936   son Carl Thomas is born; *Cori-ester* discovered

1946   Cori joins department of biochemistry, Washington University

1947   is named full professor; learns she has myelofibrosis; wins Nobel Prize with husband Carl and another researcher

1950   is named to Board of Directors, National Science Foundation

October 26, 1957   Gerty Cori dies at the age of 61

Further Reading

McHenry, Robert, ed. *Liberty's Women*. Springfield, Massachusetts: G. & C. Merriam Co., 1980. Brief description of Cori's life and accomplishments. Good source of information about other significant American women.

Opfell, Olga S. *The Lady Laureates*. New York: Scarecrow Press, 1978. Gives a detailed account of Gerty Cori's achievements, along with those of other women who have won the Nobel Prize.

Parascandola, John. "Gerty Cori." *Notable American Women*. Cambridge: Harvard University Press, 1980, pp. 165–166. This profile is short but informative.

Riedman, Sarah R., and Elton T. Gustafson. *Portraits of Nobel Laureates in Medicine and Physiology*. London: Abelard-Schuman, 1953. Offers a chance to compare the work of the Coris with that of others who won the Nobel Prize in the same field. Becomes quite technical.

Shiels, Barbara. *Winners: Women and the Nobel Prize*. Minneapolis, MN: Dillon Press, 1985. This book about Cori and other women Nobel winners was written for young readers.

Margaret Mead
(1901–1978)

Margaret Mead helped to create the new science of
anthropology.
(Photo courtesy National Archives)

What is a family? Is it a father, a mother, and their children? Or does a family include grandparents, uncles and aunts, cousins? In some places, one's family includes dead ancestors and future generations of children. Some people even count close friends.

However it is defined, the family is the basic unit of all societies. It is in families that children grow up and learn how to live their lives. Because of this, families determine what the human future will be like.

Yet scientists did not get around to studying the family until the 20th century. It was only then that the new science of *anthropology* (the study of the physical, social, and cultural lives of human beings) began. Of all the anthropologists who have considered the family since then, none was more influential than Margaret Mead.

"Marriage and family stand for a kind of human completeness," Mead once wrote, "and give individuals a sense of themselves as whole people" (Mead, *Family*, p. 78). But this happens in different ways in different human communities. People living in any particular culture tend to think that their way of rearing children is the right way, the only way. Margaret Mead believed that all people could learn from each other and that the more people knew about different kinds of families, the better the chances of building a peaceful world. Her work as an anthropologist made her feel like part of a family that stretched all the way around the earth, and she helped other Americans to think that way as well. In 1969, *Time* magazine called her "the mother of the world."

Margaret Mead was born December 16, 1901, in Philadelphia. She was the oldest of five children. One sister died as a baby. Her father was a professor at the University of Pennsylvania, and her mother was a sociologist.

Edward Sherwood Mead, Margaret's father, was a founder of the University of Pennsylvania's extension program, so he and his family lived in many different communities as he set up programs around the state. By the time Margaret reached junior high school age, she had lived in 60 different houses. All her life, Margaret found it easy to adapt to new homes and strange surroundings.

The motto of the Mead family, inherited from her grandparents, was "Do good because it is right to do good" (Howard, p. 21). All the Meads felt that it was important to live useful lives and go into professions that would benefit the human family. Margaret intended to become a sociologist like her mother until she attended Barnard College in New York City and took some classes in the new science of anthropology. Her teacher, Professor Franz Boas, said that the study of other cultures and people could free Americans from their own prejudices and give them knowledge that could be used to create a better world. This work seemed to Margaret like an exciting way to apply the Mead family motto to her own life.

In college, Margaret Mead made a group of friends that were to remain close to her throughout her life. They called themselves the "Ash Can Cats." The name came from a drama teacher who said to them, "You girls who sit up all night readin' poetry come to class lookin' like Ash Can Cats!" (Howard, p. 43). For a time, these young women shared an apartment in New York City. They stayed in touch all their lives, and probably Mead's ties to these friends helped expand her idea of the family to include people who were not blood relatives.

After graduating from Barnard in 1923, Mead went on to graduate school at Columbia University, majoring in anthropology. She also married a young seminary student named Luther Cressman. However, her interest in anthropology was too strong to allow her to settle down at that time into the role of wife and mother. When she finished her graduate studies, she wanted to do field work, which was the heart of the science of anthropology. She had been studying Polynesian culture. American Samoa seemed like a logical place for her to have her first experience of another way of life.

Mead's advisor wanted her to examine the lives of Polynesian adolescents. The time between ages 12 and 19 was a stressful, difficult period for American teenagers. Were the problems of the teens primarily due to physical changes, or were they due to the pressures of society? Margaret Mead set out to learn whether Polynesian adolescents went through the same rebellion and struggles as their American counterparts did. As a woman, Mead felt that she could have better rapport with girls than with boys, so she chose to limit her study to females.

Mead was little more than a teenager herself when she set out on this mission. Twenty-four years old, she stood not quite five feet three inches tall and weighed less than a hundred pounds. The idea of a young woman setting off alone on a 9,000-mile journey would have been shocking to most Americans in 1925, but Mead's family and friends supported her in the project. Her husband, too, thought that if this was what she wanted to do, she should do it. The long separation was not good for their marriage, though, as later events would show.

Funded by a small grant from the National Research Council, Margaret Mead set off for Samoa in the summer of 1925. She first spent some time in Hawaii, learning the language. Eventually, she was to master seven languages in addition to English. On August 31, 1925, her ship docked at the port of Pago Pago. She intended to do what anthropologists called "participant observation," in which a scientist became a part of daily life in a foreign country but also studied it.

Mead eventually settled in the village of Tau on Manua, an island 11 miles long and eight miles wide. The total population of the island was about a thousand people. There was no fresh water except rainwater caught in a tank. The houses had thatched roofs and stood on stilts over the water. There were openings between the floorboards, so that pens and other small objects were apt to roll into the sea when dropped.

She quickly developed a routine. She would get up at 5:00 A.M. and work on letter writing and paperwork until 8:00, when she began interviewing Samoans about their family histories and relationships. Lunch was eaten at noon, and then everyone went to bed for several hours to escape the worst heat of the day. At about 3:30 Margaret would do more interviews, then have supper at 5:00, and then work on until midnight. In the evenings she enjoyed having Samoan teenagers come to her house and dance for her to the music of guitars and ukeleles. These dancing sessions gave her an excellent chance to observe and get to know the young people.

Her favorite time of day was at sunset, when she and about 15 children would walk out to the shore and watch the sun go down over the sea while the waves splashed their faces.

The Samoans called Margaret "Makelita." This was an honor, for Makelita had been the last queen of Samoa. Mead quickly grew to appreciate the people's warmth and friendliness, their traditions and celebrations. Missionaries had established the Christian faith in Samoa, so the Christmas celebration was a festive one. Mead spent hours tying up little packets of soap, combs, mirrors, and hairpins to give to all the people who brought her gifts of shell and seed necklaces. The Ash Can Cats sent her a wreath that said "Home is where you hang your halo."

New Year's morning began with a storm that turned into a hurricane before the day was over. After dinner they watched the local hospital blow down, and eventually Mead and others had to climb into the water tank for safety. They crouched there in the dark in several inches of water until the wind went down. It took weeks for life on the island to get back to normal.

Mead worked frantically as she saw her remaining time on Manua dwindling. In March 1926, she wrote a letter home describing her frustration in trying to accomplish everything she wanted to do: "I'll probably leave Manua in about three weeks. And, oh, all the holes there are to patch—the width of a basket, the height of a post, the name of a feast, how they burn scars, what you really do call your mother's brother and how many fires there were at a death feast" (Mead, *Letters from the Field*, p. 55).

Letters were always an important part of Mead's life when she was in the field. Immersed as she was in this unfamiliar society, she was in danger of imagining that she could forget her own background and become a part of the culture she was studying. Letters to and from the people back home reminded her who she was. They kept her aware of her own ways of thinking and her own values, which were not the same as those of the people she now lived with. She thought of these letters as a way to keep from "drowning." In Samoa, every six weeks or so a boat would bring her 70 or 80 letters. She would spread them out on the bed, afraid at first to open them for fear of bad news that some might contain, but also anticipating the pleasure of being in touch again with her own people.

Margaret Mead left Samoa in the spring of 1926, carrying with her great quantities of notes on what she had seen and heard there. Her conclusion on the question that she had gone there to study was that the adolescent girls in Samoa had an easier time during their teens than American girls did. She decided that adolescence need not be as stressful as Western cultures made it, that growing up could be much less complicated. She felt there was a price to be paid for the Samoans' easy transition to adulthood, though; this price was "less intensity, less individuality, less involvement with life" (Howard, p. 88).

The book that came out of Mead's experience on Samoa made her famous. *Coming of Age in Samoa*, published in 1928, became a best-seller and established Mead as one of the leading anthropologists in America. She was still in her twenties.

Margaret did not immediately return to America when she left Samoa. Her husband, Luther Cressman, had been continuing his graduate studies in England, and she planned to meet him and several friends in Europe. On the long voyage from Australia to France she met Reo Fortune. Fortune was a New Zealander on his way to complete his work in psychology at Cambridge University in England. He and Margaret Mead struck up a close friendship on the trip, and she felt she had much more in common with him than she had with Cressman. A little over a year later, she and Luther Cressman agreed to divorce. Reo Fortune had kept in touch, and he had in the meantime changed his major interest from psychology to anthropology. He now suggested that he and Margaret should marry and find some kind of fieldwork they could do together.

They decided to marry in New Zealand and go on to live with the Manus people in the Admiralty Islands, a part of New Guinea. Mead wanted to do studies of children in another culture, because she felt she could not understand adolescents without studying pre-adolescents. She was especially interested in finding out how children in other cultures think. She planned to get them to draw pictures for her and to use these pictures as a way to understand how children viewed the world. With her she brought more than a thousand sheets of drawing paper. Her new husband wanted to study the Manus' religion. Once again they had to learn a new language before reaching their destination.

Some experts on child development in the 1920s believed that children were naturally creative and that if left to themselves they would show great imagination and inventiveness. Mead thought that it would make sense to test this theory in a culture like that of the Manus. Children here were allowed to play all day long. Mead's observations of them did not support the idea that children left on their own would be more creative than those given more

Margaret Mead with some Manus children during a 1928 visit to the Admiralty Islands.
(Photo courtesy UPI/Bettmann)

structure. The Manu children simply romped until they were tired, rested, and returned to their rough play.

Mead suffered from several health problems in New Guinea. She developed malaria soon after arriving, and never really recovered until their stay was over. In addition to the high fevers caused by this disease, she also broke a foot and had to get around on crutches. For some time she had been bothered by mysterious pains in her muscles, and these continued to trouble her as well.

The children went through Mead's 1,000 sheets of drawing paper in the first month. By the time she and Reo came back to the United States, she had 35,000 drawings to work with.

Mead and Fortune spent the summer of 1930 in Omaha, Nebraska, studying Native American culture. Then, in December of 1931, they returned to New Guinea. On this trip, Margaret wanted to learn how children and young people are prepared for their roles as adult men and women. She also wanted to find out whether men and women behave as they do because they are biologically different or because their cultures teach them what it means to be a man or a woman. Mead found her work with the Arapesh and Mundugumor peoples to be frustrating and felt that at first she made little progress. Finally she did get enough material to write another book about her experiences.

During her stays in the field in the 1930s, Margaret Mead was helping to develop a method of studying other cultures that would be used by anthropologists from that time on. The method involved observing, interviewing, and photographing the people among whom the scientist lived for a time. To be an effective observer, she had to know what to look for: gestures, facial expressions, rituals of celebration and mourning, interactions between parents and children, games, quarrels—all the elements of daily life in a community. To learn more about the culture through interviews, the anthropologist had to know what questions to ask and whom to talk to. Elaborate mapping systems had to be created to trace family histories and interrelationships. Photographs must be carefully labeled and dated. Objects such as carvings, jewelry, items of clothing, children's drawings and playthings must be collected and notes made about each item. Mead learned to do all this by experience and kept extensive notes on what she had learned so that it could be passed on to others.

Her next major field trip was in 1936. By this time her marriage to Reo Fortune had broken up. The isolation of fieldwork had strained their relationship, and so had Fortune's awareness that his wife's growing fame overshadowed his own reputation. Margaret now married Gregory Bateson, another anthropologist. Together they went to Bali to study mental illness in Balinese culture. There, they took hundreds of photographs and many hours of motion pictures.

Mead was still in a way inventing the science of anthropology. From Bali, she wrote: "It seems to me as if culture were rather like a cake the ingredients of which we are ignorant, and the main thing is to get a big slice home, not give it chemicals to test whether it is made of butter or oleomargarine" (Howard, p. 191).

When Mead and Bateson came back from Bali in 1938, Adolf Hitler was threatening Europe with his German armies, and Japanese power was growing in the Pacific. The world was about to plunge into a terrible war that would affect most of the countries in the South Pacific where Margaret Mead had been working. It was time to stay in the United States for a while. There was another reason to stay at home as well: after years of studying children and teenagers, Margaret Mead was expecting a baby.

Mary Catherine Bateson was born in New York City on December 8, 1939. Margaret Mead quickly discovered that being a mother was quite different from studying other people's children. Delighted with parenthood, she also found that it was impossible to be objective and scientific about her own daughter. Meeting another child of the same age, she found herself comparing him or her unfavorably to Catherine. As a scientist, she was bothered by this loss of objectivity. As a human being, she knew that motherhood made her more sensitive to the special bond between parent and child.

During the war, Bateson and Mead made their home mainly in Washington, D.C. Margaret served as head of the National Food Habits Committee. This group studied the eating habits of the American people in preparation for food rationing. Later, the committee helped to decide what kind of food, and how much, would be allowed to each family when supplies became short.

In 1953, Margaret Mead went back to Pere village in Manus, New Guinea, where she had spent most of a year in 1928–29. The children whose drawings she had brought home from the earlier trip were adults now. The islanders had much more contact with the outside world. Many of the old customs and traditions had been forgotten. People remembered Mead and welcomed her, but she found that their way of life was changing forever. Manus had been an American military base during the war, propelling the people from living in ways that were not very different from life in the stone age to the modern world in a few years. Mead told them she had returned "because of the great speed with which you have changed, and in order to find out more about how people change, so that this knowledge can be used all over the world" (Mead, *New Lives for Old*, p. 435). During her time in Pere village she helped to set up their first school.

Margaret Mead's age was making it increasingly hard for her to do the kind of fieldwork she had done earlier. She was still energetic, but now she devoted herself to teaching, lecturing, and committee work. Her classes at Columbia University were always filled with eager students who wanted to learn from the famous anthropologist.

In 1960 she broke the same ankle she had broken in 1924. She did not want to hobble around on crutches, so she bought a tall cherry wood stick with a Y-shaped fork at the top to lean on. She liked the stick so much that she kept it after the ankle healed, and it became a kind of trademark for her, along with a red cape she enjoyed wearing.

Margaret Mead had become a legend. During her last years, she was known everywhere and respected by most people as America's leading anthropologist. There were those who attacked her work as well. Some said that she relied too much on stories and not enough on factual data. Conclusions she had drawn from her field trips were questioned by others who followed her to the same place.

Whatever her limitations, Margaret Mead made a huge contribution to the understanding of human life and society. Along with a few others, she virtually invented the science of anthropology. She and those other pioneers created the methods by which later anthropologists worked.

Mead was one of those who recorded much firsthand information about cultures that had changed little over thousands of years. These cultures helped people to understand the past of all human society. Since Mead visited them, they have changed so much that many of the old ways have been abandoned, and might have been lost to human memory if not for her work.

A complete list of Mead's published writings is more than a hundred pages long. Because of the popularity of her books and articles, Margaret Mead helped Americans to realize that American society is different from, and not necessarily superior to, that of other cultures. She also promoted an awareness of the similarities that unite all humankind: its needs, its most basic values, and its home, the earth.

This may have been her greatest accomplishment. Her colleague, Barry Commoner, once said of her: "Dr. Mead's contribution to science in general—to the broad overall field of the sciences—is her pioneering work in setting the sciences into relationship to human life" (Cassidy, p. 12).

Mead's genius was not so much for digging deeply into one limited subject of scientific inquiry as it was for seeing connections and relationships. She could take in huge quantities of new information from many different sources and pull all of it together into a fresh point of view, then communicate her insights clearly to a large audience. She always wanted the things she learned to change human life for the better. Once, when asked to create her own epitaph, Mead replied that it might say: "She lived long enough to be of some use" (Cassidy, p. 156).

Mead wanted all people to learn how to bring up children who could "nest in the gale." Asked what this meant, she said that it had to do with "being able to be at home anywhere in the world, in any house, in any time band, eating any different kind of food, learning new languages as needed, never afraid of the new, sad to leave anywhere where one has been at home for a few days, but glad to go forward" (letter, Library of Congress).

This could have been a description of Margaret Mead herself. From childhood until her death on November 15, 1978 (of pancreatic cancer), she kept on traveling to strange places, meeting new people, and thinking about the meaning of all that had happened to her. She was a learner and a teacher. She cared about people all over the world and about the future of this planet. She gave her entire life to the work she began as a young woman setting sail for Samoa, and people's understanding of themselves and others is richer for it.

Chronology

December 16, 1901	Margaret Mead is born in Philadelphia
1923	graduates from Barnard College; marries Luther Cressman
1925	completes graduate work at Columbia University; goes on first field trip to Samoa
1926	returns from Samoa; divorces Luther Cressman
1928	*Coming of Age in Samoa* is published; Mead marries Reo Fortune
1928–29	works on Manus, Admiralty Islands
1931–33	works in New Guinea
1934	divorces Reo Fortune
1936	marries Gregory Bateson
1936–39	works in Bali and New Guinea
1939	gives birth to a daughter
1940–45	heads the Food Habits Committee, Washington, D.C.
1947	begins teaching anthropology at Columbia University
1953	returns to Manus
November 15, 1978	dies of pancreatic cancer

Further Reading

Works by Mead

Mead, Margaret. *Blackberry Winter*. New York: William Morrow, 1972. This autobiography deals with the early part of Mead's life.

———. *Coming of Age in Samoa: A Psychological Study of Primitive Youth for Western Civilization*. New York: William Morrow, 1928. Mead's first book.

———. *Family* (with Ken Heyman). New York: Macmillan, 1965. An interesting summary of Mead's conclusions about the importance of family in all cultures.

———. *Letters from the Field, 1925–1975*. New York: Harper & Row, 1977. This collection of Mead's letters provides details about her work in distant countries. Illustrated with her snapshots.

———. *New Lives For Old: Cultural Transformation—Manus, 1928–1953*. New York: William Morrow, 1953. Provides an account of Mead's return to Manus and describes changes that had taken place in the people's lives during the 25 years since her first work there.

Works About Mead

Emberlin, Diane. *Science: Contributions of Women*. Minneapolis, MN: Dillon Press, 1977. This book for young readers includes a 25-page profile of Mead.

Howard, Jane. *Margaret Mead: A Life*. New York: Simon and Schuster, 1984. An excellent biography. It may be too long for younger readers, but provides a wealth of information.

Ludel, J. *Margaret Mead*. New York: Watts, 1983. Concentrates mainly on Mead's fieldwork in Samoa, New Guinea, and the Admiralty Islands. An illustrated book for young readers.

Saunders, Susan. *Margaret Mead: The World Was Her Family*. New York: Viking Kestrel, 1987. A brief book for young readers emphasizing Mead's childhood and youth.

Barbara McClintock
(1902–   )

Barbara McClintock in 1980.
(Photo by Herb Parsons, courtesy Cold Spring Harbor
laboratory)

*O*ne day in the summer of 1951, Dr. Barbara McClintock read a paper at a symposium held at the Cold Spring Harbor laboratory on Long Island, New York. McClintock, a well-known geneticist, had been one of the resident researchers at the Cold Spring Harbor laboratory for 10 years, and the paper she read explained the work she had been doing for six of those 10 years. She had made an exciting discovery and was eager to tell her fellow scientists about it. But when she finished reading the paper, there was no applause. She had to go to her seat in the midst of an uncomfortable silence. Later, she heard that members of her audience had not understood what she had told them and considered it baffling, even a little crazy. One man was heard to refer to her as "just an old bag who'd been hanging around Cold Spring Harbor for years" (Keller, p. 141).

McClintock was not an overly sensitive person, but this rejection of what she considered her best work hurt. "It was just a surprise that I couldn't communicate," she said later; "it was a surprise that I was being ridiculed, or being told that I was really mad" (Keller, p. 140). Many people would have given up after such an experience, or at least lost confidence in work that had been dismissed by so many experts. Barbara McClintock simply went back to her laboratory and continued her research. It would be 30 years before the importance of these findings would be fully appreciated.

———

Barbara McClintock was born on June 16, 1902, in Hartford, Connecticut, the third daughter of Thomas Henry and Sara Handy McClintock. Her father was a family doctor struggling to establish a successful practice.

From childhood on, Barbara had an unusual independence, an ability to go her own way that sometimes confounded the people around her. As she grew older, she did not get along well with her mother, and she mystified her father. At age five she asked for a set of tools and was disappointed when she was given a child's set. She wanted *real* tools.

In 1908, when Barbara was six, the family moved to the Flatbush section of Brooklyn, which was then still a rural area. Her father had accepted a position as company doctor for the tanker crews of Standard Oil. Barbara and her sisters and brother attended the public schools there.

The McClintocks were unusual parents for that time. They encouraged each child to follow his or her interests and desires. If the children did not want to attend school, they were allowed to stay home. One year when Barbara developed a strong dislike for a teacher, her parents let her drop out of school for a whole semester. Her father refused to let his children do homework. He felt that they got enough formal education during the hours they spent at school.

Barbara enjoyed playing street games and sandlot baseball. These were the days before ready-made clothes were bought at stores. Families had a dressmaker come to the house and make their clothes. Barbara insisted on having bloomers made for her, because long skirts and dresses got in the way of her outdoor play. She was the only girl on her block's baseball team.

In high school, Barbara discovered the pleasure of learning. Science, in particular, attracted her as baseball had in childhood. "I would solve some of the problems in ways that weren't the answers the instructor expected," she later recalled. "I would ask the instructor, 'Please, let me . . . see if I can't find the standard answer' and I'd find it. It was a tremendous joy, the whole process of finding that answer, just pure joy" (Keller, p. 26).

When the United States entered the First World War in 1918, Dr. McClintock, a member of the National Guard, was called up and sent overseas as an army surgeon. This was the year of Barbara's graduation from high school, and she wanted to go on to college. However, her parents' tolerance for individual differences in their children did not extend far enough to include the idea of their daughters going to college. The oldest daughter, Marjorie, was offered a scholarship to Vassar, but Sara McClintock convinced her not to accept it. Mignon, the second daughter, also ended her formal education with high school. Sara McClintock feared that if her daughters got more education than most women had, no one would want to marry them.

With father overseas and her mother struggling to make ends meet at home, Barbara knew that there was no money for college. She took a job at an employment agency and spent her evenings reading at the public library. Then in 1919 her father came home, and with his reluctant help she persuaded her mother to let her go to Cornell University in Ithaca, New York, majoring in biology in the College of Agriculture.

She was lucky in both the time and the place of her education. Women had finally gotten the vote in 1919, and many of them now rushed to enroll at any college that would accept them. They were interested in everything, in all the studies that had been denied them for so long, and ideas about "boys' subjects" and "girls' subjects" had not yet come to dominate American schools. In 1920, the proportion of women trained in science was twice what it would be in 1970. When McClintock graduated from Cornell in 1923, 25% of the graduates of the College of Agriculture were women.

McClintock had a wonderful time during her undergraduate days at Cornell. She even played the banjo in a jazz band for a while. It was not until her junior year that she discovered the work that would occupy the rest of her life. A course in *genetics* (the biology of heredity) sparked her interest, and the professor invited her to follow that with a graduate seminar in the subject. She became a graduate student before finishing her B.S. degree in 1923.

Few fields of science were more wide open and exciting than genetics in the 1920s. The study of genetics was only a few decades old at the time. It was based on work done by an Austrian monk, Gregor Mendel, in the 19th century, but this work had not become widely known until 1900.

Mendel had grown many generations of pea plants and observed how certain traits were passed from parent plants to their offspring. Starting with purebred plants that had white flowers, he had crossed these plants with red-flowered pea plants by transferring pollen from one kind of plant to the other. All the members of the first generation of plants had red flowers, but in the second generation a fourth of the plants had white flowers. By recording the results of experiments like this, Mendel was able to see a pattern by which such traits as color were passed on. He concluded that natural laws control the ways living organisms reproduce themselves.

Then, around the turn of the century, more powerful microscopes allowed scientists to study the composition of living cells. They determined that heredity is carried in threadlike structures called *chromosomes*, and that these chromosomes are made up of *genes*, the parts of a cell that determine what any living thing will inherit from its parents. The scientists doing this work were called *cytologists*. Two of them, Nettie Stevens (see the chapter on Stevens) and Edmund B. Wilson, had identified the X and Y chromosomes that determine gender. A third, Thomas Hunt Morgan, had established a pioneering genetics laboratory at Columbia University. He and his associates studied an organism called *Drosophila* (a kind of fruit fly) to identify the chromosomes and observe their function in the development of the organism.

At Cornell, an agricultural college, studies were under way with *maize* (corn). McClintock wanted to study genetics, but women were not admitted as graduate students in the plant breeding department where most genetics courses were taught. She signed up in the botany department with a major in cytology and a minor in genetics and zoology. Soon, she became assistant to Lester Sharp, a cytology professor who encouraged her interest in plant genetics.

Dividing her time between the lecture hall, the laboratory, and the cornfield, McClintock made good use of her years as a graduate student. She earned her Ph.D. at Cornell in 1927. An invitation to stay on as an instructor and researcher let her delay any major decision about her future. She wanted to continue work already begun as a graduate student on *linkage groups* (groups of genes inherited together) in maize. McClintock hoped to find out how each linkage group related to a particular chromosome, and to discover the function of each of the 10 pairs of maize chromosomes.

She already knew the basic mechanism by which a single kernel of corn develops into a corn plant. Each cell in each kernel of corn contains the chromosomes needed to build a mature corn plant. Pollen spores from corn tassels enter the ear through the cornsilk. Cells in the pollen also contain the necessary corn chromosomes. In order for a kernel to germinate and grow into a new corn plant, a sperm cell from the pollen must unite with an egg cell in the flower. A second sperm cell unites with cells in the embryo sac to create the endosperm, which nourishes the embryo. Later, the kernel may be planted, and a new plant will develop from the embryo in the kernel.

The new plant begins with a single cell containing 10 pairs of chromosomes, half from each "parent." The original chromosomes duplicate themselves, and these pairs line up in the nucleus of the cell. Then that single cell divides, with one set of chromosomes going into one new cell and the other into the other new cell.

A corn plant must have roots; a stalk; leaves; ears; kernels; flowers, or tassels; and pollen. Throughout the growing process, the plant "knows" how to make all these parts. It is guided by information in the chromosomes. From the early 1900s on, the locations of this information within the chromosomes were called the genes. It was obvious that different genes held different information. However, although chromosomes could be seen through a microscope, no one had ever seen a gene, and geneticists did not know much about what they were or how they functioned. At the time McClintock began her work, genes were usually pictured as "beads on a string."

McClintock began by figuring out the particular function of each chromosome in maize. Each chromosome had a distinct appearance to one who studied it carefully. By observing cell divisions at various stages of a plant's development, she was able to pinpoint the job of each chromosome in the process. She grew her own corn for these studies in order to be sure exactly what she was looking at under the microscope. This meant spending long, hot hours in the fields during the summer, watching and recording the changes in each plant. At the end of the day, she liked to relax with a vigorous game of tennis.

Barbara McClintock

Between 1929 and 1931, McClintock published nine scientific papers, each a major contribution to the field of genetics. During those years she worked with an assistant, a graduate student named Harriet Creighton. In the summer of 1920, she gave Creighton a problem to work on: genetic crossover in corn, or the way in which a plant combines traits from two parents. With McClintock's advice and guidance, Creighton gathered the necessary evidence and drew some conclusions about the process.

In the spring of 1931, Morgan, the famous geneticist who had worked with Nettie Stevens, visited Cornell to give a series of lectures. On a tour of the Cornell labs he met Harriet Creighton and asked what she was working on. When she told him, he examined the data and suggested that McClintock and Creighton publish it at once. They had intended to wait for another summer's crop to confirm their findings, but with Morgan's encouragement they wrote an article that appeared in the *Proceedings of the National Academy of Sciences* in August 1931. The paper, and a presentation McClintock gave at the Sixth International Congress of Genetics the following year, helped establish her as an important geneticist and laid the groundwork for a successful career for Creighton as well.

By this time, though, McClintock realized that she had no future at Cornell. Except in the area of home economics, there were no women beyond the rank of instructor on the faculty. In 1931, McClintock was awarded a fellowship from the National Research Council. During the next two years she continued her research at Cornell and also did research at the University of Missouri and at the California Institute of Technology. She bought a Model A Ford and drove it back and forth across the country.

She was now interested in studying the *mutations* (changes in the chromosomes) that could be caused by exposure to X rays. Pollen subjected to radiation was used to fertilize corn. Future generations of this corn would then have different colors and textures. These changes helped researchers understand the workings of the chromosomes, since they could not only see the differences in the plants themselves but could also examine the chromosomes under the microscope.

One effect of X rays was breakage of many of the chromosome "threads." Observing some corn plants with odd-looking patches of color on their leaves, McClintock guessed that the variegation might be caused by "ring chromosomes." Some of the broken chromosomes probably grew back together, joining their own ends to form rings. She was later able to confirm this hunch by observing ring chromosomes under the microscope.

McClintock also identified a tiny area at the end of the sixth chromosome in maize. She named this area the *nucleolar organizer region*, or NOR, because she believed it was the place where genetic material was organized to make a mass called the nucleolus. The more she learned about the intricate workings of the corn chromosomes, the more impressed she was with the complexity of the systems they contained.

After the National Research Council fellowship ran out, McClintock won a Guggenheim fellowship for study in Germany. The time she spent there was not happy for her, although she was able to do some work at the Kaiser Wilhelm Institute in Berlin. She was horrified by the persecution of the Jews in Germany in 1933. Adolf Hitler's rise to power and the activities of the Nazis made her anxious to return to the United States, which she did as soon as possible.

Conditions in the United States were not the best then either, especially for an unemployed female geneticist. The country was in the depths of the depression, and institutions were cutting staff rather than hiring new people. She returned to Cornell, and Morgan managed to get money to fund her research there for two more years. Then another old friend, Lewis Stadler, got her a position on the faculty of the University of Missouri. Stadler was setting up a new genetics program there and was eager for the help of McClintock.

At Missouri, McClintock continued her work on the effects of X rays on the genetic makeup of corn. She published more important papers. But the job itself did not work out, for a number of reasons. Stadler's program was not part of the mainstream of activities at the University of Missouri. McClintock felt isolated from the rest of the faculty and the administration. Perhaps more important, she was impatient with rules and did not seem to think they applied to her. One Sunday, arriving at the lab without her key, she was seen climbing a wall and breaking in through a window. She and her assistant tended to ignore building hours. In the summer, she would go back to Cornell to grow her experimental corn, and if the crop was not ready in time for the beginning of school she came back late.

Such incidents contributed to a reputation McClintock developed for being "difficult." She could also be impatient with people who did not understand the importance of her work, and she sometimes expressed resentment at the lack of opportunity for advancement for women scientists. These behaviors, combined with her extreme independence and her pleasure in working alone, created the impression of a person who was not easy to work with. Her close friends knew better, but they were not always able to protect her from the negative impressions of others.

She left Missouri in 1941 after being told by her dean that she probably had no future there. Unemployed again, she went with her friend Marcus Rhoades to do some summer work at the Cold Spring Harbor laboratory on Long Island. McClintock had another friend on the staff, Milislav Demerec. Soon after McClintock's first summer there, he became director of the department of genetics and offered her a one-year position that soon became permanent. McClintock had finally found a place to work, one that would remain her headquarters for the next 50 years.

The Cold Spring Harbor laboratory was owned and operated by the Carnegie Institution of Washington. It already offered a lively genetics research program, and it was a residential as well as a research facility. During the summer, the lab hosted a variety of seminars and programs, drawing scientists from all over the world. In the winter, a small permanent staff worked on various research projects. McClintock now had everything she needed: a laboratory, a place to live, a place to grow her corn, and a salary.

McClintock could now draw on all her years of experience with maize to push her research forward in new directions. She had looked at so many corn plants in the field and so many maize chromosomes under the microscope that she knew instantly when anything unusual showed up. Her powers of observation were legendary. Once when Marcus Rhoades commented on McClintock's ability to see so much more than anyone else could see in a cell, she replied, "Well, you know, when I look at a cell I get down in that cell and look around" (Keller, p. 69).

During one season in the mid-1940s, McClintock grew some self-pollinated seedlings in which she noticed unexpected streaks or spots on the leaves. These odd patterns seemed to appear in an orderly sequence not accounted for by the X-ray treatments of the pollen. Something in the plant itself seemed to be controlling the appearance of the patterns.

Observing the plants further, McClintock noticed that many of the color patches showed up in opposite pairs. There would be more green streaks than usual on one part of a leaf and fewer than usual on another place nearby. It appeared to McClintock that the changes must have been caused by "sister cells" in the chromosomes, and that as one cell gained something its "sister" experienced an equal loss.

For six years, McClintock followed up on her original observations. Eventually she arrived at a theory she called *transposition*. According to this theory, parts of a chromosome could actually move from one position to another on the chromosome. Something McClintock called an *activator* signaled to a tiny section of the chromosome she named the *dissociator*, which then broke itself off and inserted itself into a new place on the chromosome. McClintock believed that she saw the basic material of life actually rearranging itself. This would mean that the process of heredity did not result simply from the actions of a group of preprogrammed genes that reproduced themselves. Some organized system in the material governed the way in which the plants developed.

It was this discovery, her theory of transposition, that Barbara McClintock presented to the scientists assembled at Cold Spring Harbor in the summer of 1951. It was this discovery that got the chilly reception described at the beginning of this chapter. Why?

For one thing, McClintock was out of step with the majority of researchers in her field at the time. Few geneticists continued to study complex organisms like maize. Molecular biology had for the most part replaced the older "classical" biology, and the molecular biologists wanted to study the simplest possible organisms under the microscope. Most of them worked on a simple bacterium called *E. coli*. Jacques Monod, a French Nobel Prize–winner, expressed a general belief when he said that what was true for *E. coli* would be true for the elephant. Most researchers working in the 1940s and 1950s had little or no background in corn genetics, and therefore they could not follow the proofs McClintock offered.

The discovery, in 1944, that *deoxyribonucleic acid* (DNA) was the material of heredity, had also revolutionized modern biology. Most research scientists were now following up on this important development. Many were involved in a race to discover the molecular structure of DNA (which in 1953 was proved to be a double helix). These scientists did not consider McClintock's maize studies as anything interesting.

Another problem was McClintock's isolation and her reputation as being difficult. She had been working outside the mainstream of her discipline for too long to be accepted back easily now. In fact, the transposition theory seemed so radical that it only increased her isolation.

Most important, McClintock's theory went against one of the generally accepted dogmas of biology at the time. Everyone believed that the gene was a fixed, unchanging unit of heredity and that any changes that occurred were simply random accidents. Even after the discovery of DNA, the chromosome was thought of as being like a word, made up of letters arranged in a certain order. Yet here was McClintock saying that chromosomes could rearrange themselves! It seemed absurd.

Bitterly disappointed though she was by the reception of her theory, McClintock never thought of giving up. She knew she was onto something important. During the next 30 years, she went on developing her ideas and elaborating on her theory. Meanwhile, the science of genetics gradually caught up with her.

McClintock's work did not go entirely unrecognized. In 1944, she was elected to the National Academy of Sciences, and in 1945 she served as president of the Genetics Society of America. Her reputation suffered after the 1951 paper, and it was not until 1970 that she won the National Medal of Science. By then other researchers were beginning to notice new mutations in *E. coli* that could not be explained by the old theories. Scientists began to agree that perhaps genes did move in lower life forms. Then they began to ask whether the same sort of movement could be detected in more complex forms of life—and of course, McClintock had already demonstrated that it could.

By the 1970s, McClintock had refined and expanded her basic theory. She not only said that genes could move but also that they could serve different functions in different positions on the chromosome. Also, she began to see that the controllers of these changes operated in response to stress. A plant could actually make certain changes in itself when subjected to outside forces like prolonged drought, heat, or cold.

At last the scientific community as a whole began to appreciate the brilliance of the woman they had dismissed as mistaken, old-fashioned, or crazy. Harvard gave her an honorary doctorate in 1979. In 1981 she was given the first McArthur Laureate Award, which provided an income of $60,000 a year for life, tax-free. One day later she received the Lasker Award for Basic Medical Research. Finally, in 1983, at the age of 81, Barbara McClintock won the Nobel Prize for Medicine or Physiology, becoming only the third woman to win the prize outright (without sharing it with other scientists). Her studies are now accepted as scientific fact, and no work in genetics goes on today without reference to them.

McClintock holds an ear of corn after being notified that she had received the Nobel Prize for her work with corn genetics.
(Photo courtesy UPI/Bettmann)

Asked whether she was bitter about the many years during which her work was ridiculed and ignored, McClintock replied:

Barbara McClintock

"If you know you're right, you don't care. You know that sooner or later, it will come out in the wash" (*Newsday*, October 11, 1983).

McClintock's most important work came to be known as the discovery of "jumping genes." This rather irreverent label conjures up images of little seedlike objects hopping around in cornfields—a totally inaccurate picture of the complex, invisible world she explored and mapped. The joy Barbara McClintock takes in her work goes far beyond any need for recognition or reward. To her, the life forms she has studied for so long are still mysterious and wonderful. She told an interviewer: "In the summertime, when you walk down the road, you'll see that the tulip leaves, if it's a little warm, turn themselves around so their backs are toward the sun. You can just see where the sun hits them and where the sun doesn't hit . . . " These organisms, she feels, are "fantastically beyond our wildest expectations" (Keller, p. 200).

In 1990 McClintock was still doing research at Cold Spring Harbor.
(Photo by Margot Bennett, courtesy Cold Spring Harbor laboratory)

Chronology

June 16, 1902	Barbara McClintock is born in Hartford, Connecticut
1908	family moves to Brooklyn, New York
1918	graduates from high school
1923	earns B.S. degree at Cornell University
1927	earns Ph.D. degree at Cornell; stays on as an instructor and researcher
1931	publishes paper on genetic crossover in corn; is awarded a fellowship from the National Research Council
1933	wins Guggenheim fellowship for study in Germany
1935	is appointed to the faculty of the University of Missouri
1941	joins the research staff at Cold Spring Harbor laboratory, Long Island, New York
1944	is elected a member of the National Academy of Science
1945	serves as president of the Genetics Society of America
1951	presents paper on transposition theory at Cold Spring Harbor laboratory
1970	wins National Medal of Science
1979	receives honorary doctorate from Harvard University
1981	receives the first McArthur Laureate award
1983	wins the Nobel Prize for Medicine or Physiology

Further Reading

Current Biography Yearbook. New York: H. W. Wilson Company, 1984, pp. 262–65. Gives a detailed profile of McClintock and her work.

Goldman, Martin, and Marian Gordon Goldman. "The Maverick." *Working Woman*, October, 1983, pp. 208–210. This brief popular article focuses on McClintock's scientific work as a "loner."

Keller, Evelyn Fox. *A Feeling for the Organism: The Life and Work of Barbara McClintock*. San Francisco: W. H. Freeman & Company, 1983. Although written for adults, this biography is readable and an excellent resource.

Kent, Charlotte. *Barbara McClintock*. New York: Chelsea House Publishers, 1991. A readable chronicle of McClintock's life and achievements, written for young adults.

Lewin, Roger. "Naturalist of the Genome." *Science*, October 28, 1983, pp. 402–405. Some of this material would be too technical for young readers, but parts of it provide interesting background material.

Schlessinger, Bernard and June, eds. *The Who's Who of Nobel Prize Winners*. Phoenix: Onyx Press, 1986, p. 134. A brief listing of facts and dates.

Rachel Carson
(1907–1964)

Carson became America's best-known, and most controversial, environmentalist.
(Photo by Eric Hartmann, copyrighted by Magnum Photos)

*M*oon jellies, sea pansies, ghost shrimp—these and other strange creatures of the sea became known to the millions who read Rachel Carson's best-selling books in the 1940s and 1950s. Her books are as appealing today as they were then. But it was as a prophet of environmental disaster that Carson made her most lasting contribution. She was called hysterical, unscientific, even dangerous by her critics. In the face of great opposition, Rachel Carson aroused national concern about the ecological costs of modern life.

Rachel Carson

Even the word *ecology* came into common use through Carson's writing. It comes from a Greek root meaning "house" and refers to the relationship between living things and their environment. The word had been used by biologists for many years, but it was the work of Rachel Carson that made the public aware of how fragile the earth—humanity's "house"—really is.

Rachel Carson was born May 27, 1907, in Springdale, Pennsylvania. Her father, Robert Warden Carson, had bought 65 acres of countryside as an investment, and so from the time she could toddle, Rachel was surrounded by fields, woods, and streams. Her older sister, Maria, was 10 when Rachel was born, and her brother Robert was eight. Since the other children were in school, Rachel's mother, Maria McLean Carson, had time to devote to her youngest daughter. A lover of books and nature and a former schoolteacher, Maria Carson was to be the single most important influence on Rachel's life.

Rachel Carson was a shy, reserved child who did not make friends easily. She was often ill, and her mother kept her home from school a great deal. In spite of this, Rachel was bright enough to keep up with her schoolwork easily.

Rachel Carson went to the Pennsylvania College for Women intending to be an English major and perhaps a professional writer. However, a required course in biology made her reconsider, and by her junior year she had switched to a major in zoology—against the advice of faculty members who told her that there was no future for a woman in science. At the time, Carson thought she had to make a choice between a career in writing or as a scientist. It did not occur to her that she might someday be able to combine the two.

Rachel Carson had never seen the ocean. However, she had always enjoyed reading about it and had dreamed of seeing it some day. One night she woke up in her college dormitory during a rainstorm and remembered a line from *Locksley Hall:*"For the mighty wind arises, roaring seaward, and I go." Thinking of that line of poetry, she felt as though the sea were calling to her, and indeed, most of this inlander's lifework was to be related to oceanography.

In 1929 Rachel Carson was graduated from college with a B.A. in science, magna cum laude. That summer she got her first chance to not only see the ocean but study it. She was awarded a fellowship for a summer at the Woods Hole Marine Biological Laboratory in Massachusetts. She then earned an M.A. in zoology at Johns Hopkins University, where she wrote a thesis on the development of the catfish. Much later in her life, during the controversy over her book *Silent Spring*, certain uninformed critics claimed that Carson was not a trained biologist, but she did in fact have an excellent educational background in the field. Her scholarly abilities were rewarded by a teaching post at Johns Hopkins and then at the University of Maryland, and she continued her summer studies at Woods Hole.

Rachel's father died suddenly in 1935, leaving very little money for the support of his widow. From that time until her death in 1958, Rachel provided financial support for her mother as well as herself. She needed more money than her teaching positions could provide, so she began doing part-time work for the Bureau of Fisheries in Washington, D.C.

Then the following year her older sister, Marian Williams, died at the age of 40, leaving two young daughters. Rachel and her mother decided to take the girls in and raise them. All of this happened during the depression, when money was hard to come by. With so many people depending on her, Rachel Carson needed a job with an income she could count on. She applied for a position as junior aquatic biologist with the Bureau of Fisheries. The only woman who applied for the job, she made the highest score in the competition and was hired on August 17, 1936, to work in the office of Elmer Higgins, chief of the biology division.

Carson's first job was the writing of a series of radio broadcasts called "Romance Under the Waters," which ran for a year. She then continued to write and edit bureau publications for many years. The bureau was happy to find a scientist who was also an excellent writer, able to communicate factual information in interesting and understandable ways to the general public.

Higgins suggested to Carson that she might write something general about the ocean for another radio broadcast. When he read the script, he felt it was too detailed for what he had in mind, but he suggested that she send it to the *Atlantic Monthly* instead. She did, and it was published in September, 1937, with the title "Undersea." This article brought Carson to the attention of two important people in the literary world: Quincy Howe, an editor at Simon and Schuster, and Hendrik Willem van Loon, a best-selling author. Both wrote her fan letters and encouraged her to continue writing for a popular audience.

Rachel Carson

Howe encouraged her to write a book about the ocean for Simon and Schuster. She went to work at once and spent the next four years writing *Under the Sea Wind*. Carson was a slow, careful writer. She did most of the work at night, since her days were taken up with her position at the Bureau of Fisheries. First drafts were done in longhand, at an average of about 500 words a day. A perfectionist, she rewrote each passage many times before she was satisfied. Carson had two unusual qualities that lifted her writing above the ordinary: an insistence on thorough research that gave her a wealth of factual detail to draw on and an ear for language that made her writing sing.

Her first book, *Under the Sea Wind*, appeared in 1941, just a month before the Japanese attack on Pearl Harbor. In the foreword, Carson said that the book had been written

out of the deep conviction that the life of the sea is worth knowing. To stand at the edge of the sea, to sense the ebb and the flow of the tides, to feel the breath of a mist moving over a great salt marsh, to watch the flight of shore birds that have swept up and down the surf lines of the continents for untold thousands of years, . . . is to have knowledge of things that are as nearly eternal as any earthly life can be.

The book got favorable reviews and was chosen by the Scientific Book Club as one of their selections, but it did not sell well. The outbreak of World War II overwhelmed all other concerns, and Carson, too, became involved in the war effort. She spent the year 1942–43 in Chicago, writing conservation bulletins for the government, which was concerned about the nation's food supply. In case of a meat shortage, Americans were urged to use seafood to supplement the protein in their diets. Carson's writings described various less-known seafoods and told how to prepare them.

The Bureau of Fisheries and the Biological Survey had merged in 1940 to become the Fish and Wildlife Service. Back in Washington from 1943 on, Carson continued as one of the few women employed by the service in a non-clerical position.

After the war, Carson was promoted to chief editor of all the publications of the Fish and Wildlife Service. Her new position gave her a better income and more responsibility, but it allowed less time for writing. Her mother kept house and did the cooking. Still, with two adopted nieces to raise, a demanding job, and a continuing desire to write, Carson had little room in her life for play or social activities. Asked why she had never married, she replied that she'd never had time. She enjoyed birdwatching and took a few trips with friends (always involving nature and the outdoors), but most of her energies went into her work.

A great deal of new information about the ocean became available because of the military effort in World War II. Working in the government, Carson was aware of this and wanted to make the new information available to the public. She decided to write a book that would answer the questions she had been asking all her life, a book she had looked for but never found in the library, a biography of the sea.

She began work on *The Sea Around Us* in 1948. As always, she worked slowly, gathering information from more than a thousand sources and writing letters to experts all over the world. Carson's research was not limited to reading about the sea. In the summer of 1949, she did some scuba diving in the Florida Keys. She also went on a 10-day voyage on a research boat owned by the Fish and Wildlife Service. The boat, *The Albatross*, was a converted fishing trawler, and Carson was told that no woman had ever set foot on it. She finally got permission for herself and her agent, Marie Rodell, to go along on a trip through the Georges Bank, a famous fishing area 200 miles east of Boston. All night they heard the noise of huge winches lowering cone-shaped nets to the ocean floor, then dragging them along 600 feet below the surface. Carson never forgot the sight of those nets rising into view filled with an amazing variety of ocean life: crabs, fish of all kinds, even sharks.

In June of 1949, Carson signed a contract for the book with Oxford University Press. However, she was still not finished writing it, and problems at home slowed the work. One of her nieces became seriously ill, and Carson had to take a month off. Then the whole family moved into a new house in Silver Spring, Maryland. Finally, in July of 1950, the manuscript went to the publisher. Parts of it were also submitted to various magazines, but at first they were rejected by one publication after another. Eventually, the *Yale Review* took a chapter, and *The New Yorker* agreed to publish half of the manuscript before it came out in book form.

The success of *The Sea Around Us* was assured when the magazine excerpts appeared. The chapter in the *Yale Review* won the George Westinghouse Science Writing Award, and the response to the three parts in *The New Yorker* was the greatest that magazine had ever received. The book itself was finally published on July 2, 1951. It was chosen by the Book of the Month Club and immediately made the best-seller list, where it remained for 86 weeks. Alice Roosevelt Longworth, daughter of former president Theodore Roosevelt, stayed up all night reading it, and then at 5:00 A.M. started reading through it again. Her fascination was typical of the huge public response to the book.

The Sea Around Us eventually won both the John Burroughs Medal and the National Book Award. It sold a quarter of a million copies in the first year. And it made Rachel Carson famous.

Of course she enjoyed the book's success, and the money it earned eased her financial worries for the first time in years. Still, Rachel Carson was not the sort of person who wanted to be a celebrity. She did not know how to react when she received marriage proposals from strange men or was approached on the street by fans. Some of the letters she got amused her; for instance, one man addressed her as "Dear Sir" even though he knew she was a woman because he could not believe any woman could be intelligent enough to have written that book. Still, she was too shy to be comfortable with her sudden fame.

Even before the publication of *The Sea Around Us*, Carson had begun work on a new book. Now, her new financial independence allowed her to do more than dream of being a full-time writer. On June 3, 1952, she resigned from her post at the Fish and Wildlife Service.

The new book was to be called *The Edge of the Sea*. Carson had gotten the idea from Rosalind Wilson, an editor at Houghton Mifflin. Wilson had been walking along the beach one day when she saw a lot of horseshoe crabs that appeared to be stranded on the sand. After doing a "good deed" by throwing them all back into the ocean, she learned that she had interrupted their normal mating activities. Embarrassed by her own ignorance, Wilson suggested that Carson write a book about life along the shore.

The money from *The Sea Around Us* also allowed Carson to buy land in Maine, overlooking Sheepscot Bay. There, in 1953, she had a summer cottage built overlooking the bay. It was a perfect place to research the New England portion of the new book. She could go out at all times of the day and night, exploring the tidal pools along the shore with a magnifying glass. From the cottage window, she could watch seals and whales at the mouth of the harbor. With the book's illustrator, Bob Hines, she traveled to North Carolina and Florida to research the other parts of the book. He sometimes had to carry her out of the icy water because she stayed so long her legs became numb. She would bring buckets of living creatures to Hines for him to draw, and then she would return them to the water. Unable to remember the names of all these organisms, he called them her "wee beasts."

Rachel Carson enjoyed bird-watching in her spare time.
(Photo by Eric Hartmann, copyrighted by Magnum Photos)

The Edge of the Sea was published in 1955 and became another best-seller. In it, Carson emphasized how fragile and interdependent the life along the ocean shore was. The book did more than name and describe the creatures of the shore; it made its readers feel the wonder and mystery of these ancient forms of life.

Rachel's mother, Maria, was now in her late eighties, and crippled with arthritis. Her niece Marjorie, now an adult and the mother of a son, Roger, also developed severe arthritis and came to Maine to stay. Then in 1957 Marjorie died suddenly of pneumonia. Once again Rachel stepped in, taking over as the mother of a five-year-boy. In 1958 Maria Carson died, leaving Rachel alone with her new son. All these family troubles left her little time or energy for writing. She published a few articles in the late 1950s and wrote a television program about the sky for *Omnibus*.

Like *The Edge of the Sea*, the idea for Rachel Carson's last and most famous book was suggested by a friend. Olga Owens Huckins and her husband owned a private bird sanctuary in Duxbury, Massachusetts. One day a plane few over it spraying DDT for mosquito control, and the next morning the Huckins' found seven dead songbirds. The birds had obviously died in agony. Their beaks were wide open and their claws clutched horribly against their bodies. Outraged, Mrs. Huckins wrote a letter of protest to the Boston *Herald*, and she sent a copy to Rachel Carson.

Carson had long been concerned about the indiscriminate spraying of DDT and other pesticides. As long ago as 1945, she had tried to persuade *Reader's Digest* to publish an article about the dangers of these substances to the environment, but the *Digest* had not been interested. Since that time, use of poisons developed during World War II had risen dramatically, and many scientists were worried about the unknown effects of these materials.

The letter from Olga Huckins encouraged Carson to start investigating the problem. She later wrote that "the more I learned about the use of pesticides the more appalled I became . . . everything which meant most to me as a naturalist was being threatened" (Brooks, p. 233). She again approached *Reader's Digest* about an article and was again turned down. She tried other magazines with equally negative results. No one wanted to touch the subject.

In May of 1957, part of Long Island had been drenched with DDT in an attempt to eradicate the gypsy moth. A group of citizens sued the government, and the resulting trial produced a great deal of evidence of the damage that could be caused by pesticides. Even though the lawsuit failed because of a legal technicality, Carson's study of the transcripts increased her sense of urgency. Finally in

May of 1958 she convinced Houghton Mifflin to sign a contract with her for a book about the problem.

DDT had been known since 1874, but it had not been used as a pesticide until 1939, when it was used in Switzerland to save a potato crop. During the Second World War, it was dusted on people to kill body lice that carried deadly typhus microorganisms. When the government made it and other chemicals available to the general public after the war, farmers and home gardeners rushed to buy the "miracle" powders and sprays that would keep insects from destroying their crops. Local governments started spreading the poisons to control mosquitoes and other annoying insects. A huge advertising campaign promoted the new products. By 1958, when Carson began looking into the problem, almost 200 million dollars worth of pesticides were being sold each year; DDT and similar products were big business.

Few people seemed to be asking the questions Carson wanted to ask: What was all this spraying of poisons doing to the delicate balance of nature? Were "good" insects being destroyed along with the "bad"? What were the effects on birds, fish, and other wildlife? And what might the long-term effects be on humans who consumed food and water tainted by the pesticides? One of the many alarming facts Carson discovered in her research was that between 1932 and 1951, the amount of arsenic (a dangerous poison) found in American tobacco plants had increased 300%. This was before the other harmful effects of smoking had been established, but the idea of millions of Americans smoking cigarettes laced with that much arsenic was cause for concern.

The subject was large and complicated. Many scientists had noted alarming changes in the environment, but no one had attempted to put all the evidence together. Even if that were accomplished and the huge jigsaw puzzle produced a threatening picture, it seemed unlikely that anything could be done about it. Business, government, and the public had reasons for using pesticides. Only a trained scientist who was well known, respected, and extremely persuasive could hope to convince people that changes must be made.

Carson recognized the difficulty of the job she had taken on. She knew the resistance she would be facing and described it accurately: "This is an era of specialists, each of whom sees his own problems and is unaware or intolerant of the larger frame into which it fits. It is also an era dominated by industry, in which the right to make a dollar at whatever cost is seldom challenged" (Sterling, p. 148). She also said that she knew "there would be no peace for me if I kept silent" (Brooks, p. 228).

As always, Carson worked hard to get the facts before writing anything. She contacted every expert she could locate, combed the files at the Fish and Wildlife Service, and patiently accumulated information on what was known about the effects of pesticide use, not only in the United States, but worldwide. Professor George J. Wallace of Michigan State University documented an alarming decline in the bird population on that campus after a spraying for Dutch elm disease. Dr. M. M. Hargraves of the Mayo Clinic helped Carson document medical aspects of the subject. Dr. Wilhelm C. Hueper of the National Cancer Institute confirmed Carson's suspicion that the widespread use of pesticides in-creased cancer risks in humans.

The subject of cancer was also a personal concern as Rachel Carson worked on her book. Early in 1960 she had a breast tumor removed. When she asked, she was told that it was not malignant. However, by the end of the year she learned that the doctors had tried to spare her feelings by giving her false assurances. The cancer had spread, and she now began radiation treatments. She thought of her own cancer as something that had gone wrong with the ecology of her body's cells.

The illness delayed work on the book, but finally, after two years of work, *Silent Spring* was finished. On June 16, 1962, a conden-sation appeared in *The New Yorker*. Within a week a storm of controversy had broken out. The chemical companies and the U.S. Department of Agriculture attacked the book in a major public relations campaign that ignored the factual basis of the book and ridiculed Carson as a nonscientific, emotional crank.

The attacks continued and increased when the full book was published the following September. Dr. Frederick T. Stare of the School of Public Health at Harvard called the book "baloney." The review published in *Time* magazine said it was "unfair, one-sided, and hysterically overemphatic" (*Time*, September 8, 1962). *Reader's Digest* canceled its plans to run a condensation and instead published a short version of the *Time* article. Dr. Robert White-Stevens of the American Cyanamid Company be-came the main spokesman for the industry, claiming that if the United States paid attention to Carson's warnings it would return to the Dark Ages.

But *Silent Spring* had its supporters as well, and as time went on it became evident that many of the attacks on the book were based on a misinterpretation of its contents. For instance, Carson never suggested that all pesticides should be banned. She urged that control and distribution of these substances should be given to biologists who could make informed decisions about the risks involved. She also favored the development of biological controls as alternatives to the sprays.

Gradually, the tide of public opinion turned in spite of the efforts to discredit the author of *Silent Spring*. By the end of 1962 there were more than 40 bills in state legislatures for the regulation of pesticides, and the following summer Carson was asked to testify before two Senate committees. Secretary of the Interior Steward Udall worked hard to change government policies as a result of the Carson book, and in Great Britain Prince Philip recommended the book widely. And the time came when DDT was banned throughout the United States. In November 1969, the United States government took action to phase out the use of DDT over a two-year period.

Carson did not view this as the solution to all environmental problems—far from it. She was already concerned about the careless disposal of radioactive wastes, the industrial pollution of air and water, and many other issues that affect life on earth. Believing that 20th-century civilization was too complex to be addressed only by specialists working in isolation, she foresaw a new science of what she called "biotic controls" in which entomologists, pathologists, geneticists, physiologists, biochemists, and ecologists would cooperate to collect and interpret information and then influence public policy. If she had lived longer, she might have been one of the founders of such a new science.

Rachel Carson received many awards in the last year of her life, but she was often too ill to attend the ceremonies. In March of 1963, she wrote in a letter: "Oh—at long last, the first thin bubble of frog song came from the swamp Sunday night, after a warm, sunny day. And last evening I heard the first robin song. So spring is not to be silent!" (Brooks, p. 319).

She faced her own death calmly. Having spent so many years studying the life cycles of nonhuman creatures, it did not seem strange to her that her own life cycle should also have its end. The response to *Silent Spring* assured her that she had done what she could to preserve the natural world she loved, and on April 14, 1964, at the age of 56, she left it.

Rachel Carson was one of those rare scientists who are also gifted with the ability to write with beauty and passion. Because of this gift, she had a unique opportunity to persuade the American public that it had taken a dangerous course. She became one of the true prophets of the 20th century, and the concerns she raised still trouble the United States and the world.

In Maine in 1970, the Rachel Carson National Wildlife Refuge was dedicated to her memory.

Carson once wrote an article for parents called "Teach Your Child to Wonder." In it, she described exploring the backyard at night with a flashlight as an activity by which parents might nurture the "sense of wonder" in their children. It was that sense of wonder and awe at the constant discoveries open to an observer of nature that Carson communicated so well to her readers. One who sees the beauty and mystery of life on earth will not want to destroy it.

The Sea Around Us concluded with a sentence that could serve as an appropriate epitaph for Rachel Carson: "For all at last return to the sea—to Oceanus, the ocean river, like the ever-flowing stream of time, the beginning and the end."

Chronology

May 27, 1907	Rachel Carson is born at Springdale, Pennsylvania
1929	earns B.A. in science, Pennsylvania College for Women
1932	earns M.A. in zoology, Johns Hopkins University
1935	Carson's father dies; Carson begins work at the Bureau of Fisheries
1937	"Undersea" is published in *Atlantic Monthly*
1941	*Under the Sea Wind*, Carson's first book, is published
1949	Carson appointed editor-in-chief for the Fish and Wildlife Service
1951	*The Sea Around Us* is published
1952	*The Sea Around Us* wins National Book Award
1955	*The Edge of the Sea* is published
1957	Carson's niece, Marjorie, dies suddenly; Carson adopts her five-year-old son
1958	Rachel's mother, Maria McLean Carson, dies
1960	Carson had tumor removed; is told she has cancer
1962	*Silent Spring* is published; arouses controversy
April 14, 1964	Rachel Carson dies
1970	Rachel Carson National Wildlife Refuge is dedicated in Maine

Further Reading

Works by Carson

Carson, Rachel. *The Edge of the Sea*. Boston: Houghton Mifflin, 1955. One of Carson's most popular books, this description of the seashore from Maine to Florida includes more than 160 illustrations by Bob Hines.

———. *The Sea Around Us*. New York: Oxford University Press, 1951. This was the book that made Carson famous.

———. *Silent Spring*. Boston: Houghton Mifflin, 1962. One of the most controversial books ever published in America, it was also one of the most influential. Young readers might become bogged down in the technical data, but could read parts of it with interest and understanding.

Works About Carson

Anticaglia, Elizabeth. "Rachel Carson." *Twelve American Women*. Chicago: Nelson-Hall, 1975. Includes a 16-page biography of Rachel Carson.

Brooks, Paul. *The House of Life: Rachel Carson at Work*. Boston: Houghton Mifflin, 1972. Brooks was one of Carson's editors, and a friend. Focuses on Carson's methods of researching and writing her books; includes excerpts from her writings.

Gartner, Carol B. *Rachel Carson*. New York: Frederick Ungar, 1983. Emphasizes Carson's literary achievements. Probably too difficult for younger readers.

"The Gentle Storm Center." *Life*, October 12, 1962, p. 105. Picture story about the battle over *Silent Spring*.

Jezer, M. *Rachel Carson*. New York: Chelsea House, 1988. This young adult biography presents a readable portrait of Carson. Includes a bibliography.

Sterling, Philip. *Sea and Earth: The Life of Rachel Carson*. New York: Thomas Y. Crowell, 1970. An interesting and well-researched portrait of Rachel Carson intended for young readers.

Rosalyn Yalow
(1921–)

*Rosalyn Yalow and her collaborator, Solomon Berson,
developed a sensitive biological technique called
radioimmunoassay (RIA).*
(Photo courtesy of Dr. Rosalyn Yalow)

"**W**hether we like it or not, women, even now, must exert greater total effort than men for the same degree of success" (Opfell, p. 229). Rosalyn Yalow knew what she was talking about when she wrote those words. Starting out not only as a female but also as the child of a poor family, she had achieved the highest possible degree of success in science. She had done it through sheer talent and intelligence, and through extraordinary effort. One of the hopes she expressed after winning the Nobel Prize was that she and other prominent women scientists could make things easier for the next generation.

Yalow's concern about equal rights for women is more than a personal desire for fairness. She believes that denial of opportunity creates a terrible waste: "The world cannot afford the loss of the talents of half its people if we are to solve the many problems which beset us" (Vare, p. 132).

Knowing of this concern, some people were surprised when Rosalyn Yalow spoke out in support of Allan Bakke, a young man who sued a medical school for discrimination. Bakke claimed that minorities and women were favored over white males in the school's admission policies and that this was just as unfair as the long tradition of discrimination against women and racial minorities. Yalow agreed. She argued that if women demanded special consideration they were in a sense agreeing with those who said they could not compete on their own merits. Equal opportunity would be enough, and that should be the goal. This opinion angered some of her fellow feminists, but Rosalyn Yalow had never let others tell her what to think.

She was born Rosalyn Sussman on July 19, 1921, in the South Bronx area of New York City. In the 1920s, as now, living in the Bronx could mean poverty, hard work, and unequal opportunities. Her father, the son of Russian Jewish immigrants, had a small paper and twine business. Her mother had come to the United States from Germany at the age of four. Neither Simon nor Clara Sussman had been educated beyond grade school, but they were determined that their children, Rosalyn and her brother Alexander, would go to college.

When the depression of the 1930s began, times were even harder in the Bronx. The Sussmans always had food and shelter, but there was no money for extras.

Rosalyn attended Public School 51, Public School 10, and Walton High School in the Bronx. An excellent student, she filled out what was missing in her education by reading on her own. From the time she was five years old, she and her brother went to the New York Public Library every Saturday and carried home armloads of books for the week. In high school, Rosalyn's special loves were mathematics and chemistry.

After high school she enrolled at Hunter, part of the system called the City College (now University) of New York. Qualified students could attend Hunter tuition free. The Sussmans hoped that their daughter would become an elementary school teacher, but Rosalyn loved the sciences, especially physics. By 1941, when she graduated from Hunter at the age of 19, she was determined to become a physicist.

Physics was an exciting field at the time, with important discoveries being made regularly. The new area of nuclear physics especially attracted Rosalyn Sussman. She had heard a lecture by Italian scientist Enrico Fermi, who had won the 1938 Nobel Prize in Physics for his atomic research, and had read Eve Curie's biography of Marie Curie, a discoverer of natural radioactivity.

In order to do graduate work in physics, Rosalyn would need a teaching assistantship to pay her tuition and support her while she took her classes. Prospects did not look good. Despite her outstanding college record, she expected to have trouble competing with graduates of more prestigious universities for the few assistantships that were available. Hunter had just started its physics major; in fact, Rosalyn was the first graduate. And she was a woman.

The wife of one of her college professors told her of a well-known biochemist at Columbia University who needed a secretary. Perhaps a job like that might lead to an opportunity for graduate education—but she would have to learn shorthand. Rosalyn took the job, and after she graduated from Hunter she enrolled in a business college.

The United States had just entered World War II, and America's young men were subject to the draft. Suddenly the number of male applicants for teaching assistantships went down drastically. Rosalyn got an offer of an assistantship from the University of Illinois in February 1941. She accepted and dropped out of business college. In June she quit her secretarial job and took two physics courses in summer school. That fall, Rosalyn Sussman went off to Champaign-Urbana to begin graduate work in physics.

As a teaching assistant, she attended the first faculty meeting of the College of Engineering—and found that she was the only woman among some 400 male faculty. She was told that she was the first female to receive an assistantship in the physics department since 1917.

On her first day at the University of Illinois, Rosalyn also met a fellow student named Aaron Yalow. At first he made fun of her

New York accent, but they quickly became friends. Aaron was also starting work toward a doctorate in physics.

The first year was hard. Because of the limitations of Hunter College's curriculum, Rosalyn had taken less coursework than most of the other graduate students. In her first year she audited (took without getting a grade or credit) two undergraduate courses to try to catch up, took three graduate courses for credit, and taught freshman physics half-time. Despite this grueling schedule, she received A's in all her courses, with an A– in lab. The department chairman commented that the A– proved that women could not do well in laboratory work.

In 1943, Rosalyn and Aaron Yalow were married. By this time Rosalyn had begun work on her thesis, which involved research in nuclear physics. Her thesis director, Dr. Maurice Goldhaber, gave her much help and encouragement. So did his wife, Dr. Gertrude Goldhaber, who was also a distinguished physicist but could not teach at the University of Illinois because university rules prohibited a husband and wife from receiving two university salaries. Such rules were common. They meant that Rosalyn and Aaron Yalow probably could not both become university professors, at least not at the same university.

As she worked on her thesis, Yalow learned how to use instruments that measured radioactive substances, even in tiny amounts. Her field of interest was nuclear physics. At this time, in the middle of World War II, some of the top scientists in the United States were working to create an atomic bomb that could bring victory and end the war. Rosalyn received her Ph.D. in nuclear physics a few months before the first atomic bombs were dropped on Hiroshima and Nagasaki in August of 1945. A tremendous new force had been let loose in the world. Yalow wanted to help find ways to use this power to help rather than destroy people.

After graduation, Rosalyn Yalow became an assistant engineer at the Federal Telecommunications Laboratory back in New York City. In the following year she returned to Hunter College to teach physics to returning war veterans. But her strongest interest was still in research, especially research involving the use of radioactive materials.

At this time Aaron was employed as a medical physicist at Montefiore Hospital in the Bronx. He introduced Rosalyn to Dr. Edith Quimby, an outstanding physicist at the Columbia University College of Physicians and Surgeons (see chapter on Edith

Quimby in this book). Rosalyn then volunteered to work in Dr. Quimby's laboratory in order to get experience with medical uses of radioactivity. Through Dr. Quimby she met Dr. Giaocchino Failla, who knew that the Veteran's Administration Hospital in the Bronx needed someone to help set up a radioisotope service there. He recommended Yalow for the job.

Some background information may be helpful in understanding Rosalyn Yalow's work. An atom is a tiny particle of matter with a nucleus at its center surrounded by rings of electrons, or negatively charged particles. The nucleus is made up of other small particles, called protons and neutrons. Protons have a positive charge; neutrons are neutral. Atoms—the smallest units an element can be reduced to and still retain its properties—are the building blocks of all matter. They are usually stable.

At the end of the 19th century Marie Curie, together with her husband Pierre and another scientist, Henri Bequerel, had discovered that some materials are naturally *radioactive* (that is, their atoms are unstable and emit penetrating rays). In 1934 Marie Curie's daughter, Irene, together with her husband, Frederick Joliot, discovered that they could make normally stable substances radioactive. Now researchers wanted to know more about how radioactive materials could be used in treating disease.

Rosalyn Yalow started work at the VA Hospital as a part-time consultant. Between 1947 and 1950 she developed and equipped the new radioisotope service, starting work in a converted janitor's closet. At first, the only funds available came from a small grant provided by a veterans' group. Yalow built some of her own equipment, and in the early years, together with physicians in the radiology department, she carried out several research projects and published the findings.

In 1950, the research seemed so exciting that Yalow left her teaching job and went to work for the VA full time. In the same year, a young physician named Solomon A. Berson completed his residency at the hospital and joined the Radioisotope Service. Yalow and Berson began a professional partnership that lasted for the next 22 years. They worked well together. Berson had the training and expertise of a physician, and Yalow that of a research scientist. As she put it: "He wanted to be a physicist, and I wanted to be a medical doctor" (Opfell, p. 230). Together, they began to investigate ways to use the new knowledge provided by nuclear physics to understand how the body functions in health and in disease.

Rosalyn Yalow

Rosalyn and Aaron Yalow had a son, Benjamin, in 1952, and a daughter, Elanna, in 1954. Rosalyn took a week off work for each birth. The Yalows believed that it was possible for both of them to have demanding careers and still have a family. They could afford to hire a live-in helper who cared for the children, and Rosalyn's mother also helped out when the children were pre-schoolers. "I've always had time for my children," Rosalyn Yalow said in an interview after she won the Nobel Prize. "I went home every day for lunch. When the children were small, if I worked on weekends, they came to the laboratory with me. When they were older, I took them to museums, on trips . . . " (Kent, p. 174).

Yalow and Berson began their most ambitious work with a study of how radioactive iodine could be used to diagnose thyroid disease. They and others used radioactive iodine to treat overactive thyroids and thyroid cancer.

They then began a study of the body's use of the hormone insulin. An understanding of this was important for the treatment of diabetes, a disease in which the body does not make enough insulin. Insulin is needed to store and burn the sugar in food. Some diabetics must put insulin into their bodies, usually by injection, in order to function normally. Insulin injections had been used to treat diabetes since the 1920s.

In attempting to learn how diabetics used insulin, Yalow and Berson injected radioactive iodine–labeled insulin and found that adult diabetics produced *antibodies* (proteins that guard the body against foreign substances) that slowed down their ability to use the life-giving insulin. In studying this reaction, the two scientists found a way to use substances tagged with radioactive *isotopes* (atoms, the nuclei of which have the same number of protons but different numbers of neutrons, thus they are different forms of the same element) and their antibodies to measure traces of substances such as insulin in the blood. They called their method radioimmunoassay (RIA).

This procedure begins with the injection of a substance to be measured into laboratory animals such as rabbits or guinea pigs. The animals develop antibodies to fight against this foreign substance. Carefully measured amounts of these antibodies are then mixed in test tubes with radioactively labeled *antigen* (the substance producing the immune response). A chemical reaction takes place. After a certain amount of time, scientists can determine the amount of any specific substance in the blood by comparing the makeup of the mixture from the test tube with a standard curve. Computers can be used to speed up the necessary calculations.

The RIA test is so sensitive that it can detect amounts as small as a billionth of a gram. It soon became clear that this same test could be used to measure all kinds of substances in human blood—other hormones, enzymes, vitamins. Scientists could use RIA to understand how the body functions and to help identify the causes of some diseases. RIA could measure amounts so tiny that someone later compared it to finding a lump of sugar in a lake 62 miles long and 30 feet deep.

Yalow and Berson first reported their discovery in 1959. Within six years RIA was widely used by scientists and medical doctors. Questions about this procedure came in from all over the world, and Yalow became head of an RIA reference laboratory at the VA Hospital in 1966.

In 1968, Sol Berson was named chairman of the department of medicine at Mount Sinai School of Medicine. Yalow was appointed acting chief of the radioisotope service at the VA Hospital when he left. Four years later, Berson died suddenly. Rosalyn Yalow named her new laboratory at the VA Hospital the Solomon A. Berson Research Laboratory in his honor.

She missed working with Berson, but the Veteran's Administration continued to fund her research. Through the years Berson and Yalow, and now Yalow alone, were interested in training young researchers. She calls them her "professional children."

On October 13, 1977, Rosalyn Yalow was already at work at her desk when at 7:00 A.M. she received a call from Stockholm, Sweden. Together with two other researchers (who had used RIA in their work), she had been awarded the Nobel Prize in Physiology or Medicine. The Nobel committee said that her discovery had "brought about a revolution in medical research" (Vare, p. 130). RIA's ability to measure tiny amounts of substances had made more difference in medical research than any technique since the X ray.

"For the first hour," Yalow said later, "I had no reaction—I was absolutely stunned" (Opfell, p. 226). Then her telephone began ringing, and her office filled up with flowers. Her husband Aaron, who was now a physics professor at Cooper Union, and their son, Benjamin, a computer programmer, came to congratulate her. Daughter Elanna called from California, where she was a doctoral student at the time. Yalow's only regret was that Sol Berson was not there to share the prize with her.

Rosalyn Yalow

In her acceptance speech, Yalow challenged young women to become scientists and use their talents to benefit all people: "We must believe in ourselves," she said, "or no one else will believe in us" (Vare, p. 131).

Since 1977, Rosalyn Yalow has continued to work on the applications of RIA and on other related research. RIA has proven useful in diagnosing high blood pressure, tuberculosis, and some forms of cancer in addition to its importance in understanding diabetes. Because it requires radioactive materials, Yalow has also been interested in promoting the safe and peaceful use of nuclear energy. She has published several articles pointing out that people

Rosalyn S. Yalow won the Nobel Prize in 1977.
(Photo courtesy of Dr. Rosalyn Yalow)

are much more likely to get cancer and other diseases from smoking than from nuclear accidents—yet many people continue to smoke. Yalow feels that *nuclear* has become almost a bad word because people do not distinguish between nuclear war and nuclear power. Recently, a new imaging technique based on nuclear magnetic resonance was named MRI (for magnetic resonance imaging) rather than the logical NMRI because radiologists did not want to associate their technique with the word *nuclear*. Yet Yalow's work has demonstrated that knowledge and use of radioactive substances can offer great benefits if handled properly.

The importance of RIA has now been clearly recognized. Researchers are still finding new uses for the technique. For example, the medical examiners have used RIA to detect small amounts of poison in corpses. A recent adaptation of the test called RIAH is used on human hair to identify drugs in the hair proteins. Hair retains a permanent record of drug abuse, so RIAH may supplement or even replace urinalysis as a drug testing method.

Rosalyn Yalow was the first woman since Gerty Cori to win a Nobel Prize in Physiology or Medicine, and she was only the sixth woman to win in any science category in the history of the Nobel awards. Since 1977 three additional women have received Nobel Prizes in science, including another Hunter College graduate. Yalow believes that with equal opportunity for a good education and equal encouragement to enter all fields of work, women will someday make even greater contributions to the sciences. She looks forward to a time when all "those of us who wish can reach for the stars" (Opfell, p. 233).

Chronology

July 19, 1921	Rosalyn Sussman is born in New York City
1941	graduates from Hunter College, New York City
1942	receives M.S., University of Illinois
1943	marries Aaron Yalow
1945	receives Ph.D., University of Illinois
1946	teaches physics at Hunter College
1947	begins part-time work as a consultant, Veterans' Administration Hospital, Bronx, New York City
1950	resigns from Hunter; begins full-time work, VA Hospital
1952	has a son, Benjamin
1954	has a daughter, Elanna
1959	Yalow and Berson publish study on reaction between insulin and its antibody
1966	Yalow named head of RIA reference laboratory
1968	Berson leaves VA Hospital; Yalow named acting chief, radioisotope service
1970	is named chief of Nuclear Medicine Service, VA Hospital
1972	longtime professional partner Sol Berson dies
1976	Yalow wins the Albert Lasker Award for basic medical research. First woman to win this prize
1977	wins the Nobel Prize in Physiology or Medicine

Further Reading

Bernstein, Fred A. *The Jewish Mothers' Hall of Fame.* New York: Doubleday, 1986, pp. 70–75. Offers a brief sketch of Yalow's life and work, along with many other interesting profiles.

Kent, Letitia. "Winner Woman!" *Vogue*, Jan. 1978, p. 131, 174–75. A popular article recognizing Yalow's achievement in winning the Nobel Prize. Based on an interview.

McHenry, Robert, ed. *Liberty's Women.* Springfield, Massachusetts: G & C Merriam Co., 1980. Describes the careers of many prominent American women, including Rosalyn Yalow.

Opfell, Olga S. *The Lady Laureates.* New York: Scarecrow Press, 1978. Gives a lengthy and readable account of Yalow's work, focusing on the Nobel Prize–winning development of the RIA technique. Material on other female Nobel winners.

Vare, Ethlie Ann, and Greg Ptacek. *Mothers of Invention.* New York: William Morrow, 1988. Presents brief notes on many American women with scientific and technical achievements; Yalow is included.

Mildred Dresselhaus
(1930–   )

*Mildred Dresselhaus was the first woman elected president
of the American Physical Society.*
(Photo courtesy Massachusetts Institute of Technology)

Some day high-speed trains may carry passengers in and out of
American cities, not running on tracks but suspended above
guideways by magnetic forces. SQUIDs (superconducting quantum interference devices) are already being used to locate oil,
water, and mineral deposits that cannot be found by traditional
methods; these devices will be employed in the future in many
other fields from medicine to space communications. Computers
will continue to become faster and more sophisticated through
new technology.

All these advances, and many others, will be made possible through the work of scientists in the field of *solid state physics* (the study of solid, rather than gaseous or liquid, materials). A leader in this area of research for more than 30 years, Mildred Dresselhaus has devoted her efforts to the scientific issues behind the techniques that allow solid materials to be used in new ways.

Mildred Spiewak was born on November 11, 1930, in Brooklyn, New York. Mildred started life with some important advantages. She was born into a close family that recognized her talents and wanted her to get an education and have a career. Naturally intelligent, she had a gift for mathematics and abstract thinking. And her early life taught her not to be afraid of hard work.

These advantages offset the difficulties she had to overcome, but there were some serious obstacles blocking her way. Her family was poor. Her parents had come to the United States as immigrants with no money and very little education. They settled in New York City at the beginning of the depression of the 1930s.

In those days even long-established American families had a hard time paying their bills. Mildred's parents found whatever jobs they could and managed to put food on the table, at least for the children. At one time Mildred and her brother had just one set of clothes and one pair of shoes each. They both went to work as soon as they were old enough to find something that would add a few dollars to the family income. When she was 11, Mildred tutored a mentally re-tarded child three hours a day, five days a week. During the year when she had this job, Mildred was paid 50 cents a week.

Education was seen as the best way out of the slums of Brook-lyn. Luckily, both children loved school and did well in their schoolwork. They also enjoyed music. By the time Mildred's brother was six years old, he was playing in a local orchestra. Both of them had enough talent to get free music lessons.

Although she enjoyed learning, Mildred had a difficult time with the social aspects of New York City's schools. She went to such a rough junior high school that she never once used a bathroom there because the bathrooms were not safe. Girls were often attacked there. Mildred was beaten up many times on her way to and from school, but eventually she learned how to protect herself and avoid dangerous situations. Still, it was hard to make the most of education when she had to use so much energy on sheer survival.

Mildred's greatest gift seemed to be for mathematics. Her parents hoped that she might be able to go to college and become a teacher, but there was no money for college fees.

Luckily, New York City had a fine college, Hunter, that offered free tuition to bright young people. Hunter even ran a high school to prepare students for college. This high school restricted its student body to the best applicants only and gave a difficult entrance exam to decide who would be accepted. Mildred's neighborhood junior high had not given her a very strong background. Her parents, with their poor English and lack of education, could not help her. She studied alone and passed the test, earning a perfect score in math. Later, she said that nothing she did in the rest of her life was as hard as getting ready for that high school examination.

Hunter High had much higher standards than her old school did. Again, she had to work hard on her own to keep up. During her first semester she got poor grades on many papers, but soon after that Mildred was again at the top of her class. She developed an interest in the sciences that would last a lifetime.

After graduating from high school in 1947, Mildred was determined to go on to college. Hunter seemed to be the only possible choice, with its free tuition. She won a state scholarship that would pay most of her other expenses. She also set up a small tutoring business at Hunter so she could continue to contribute to her family's expenses.

The freshman physics course at Hunter gave Mildred her life work. Here was a science where she could use both her math skills and her abilities as an abstract thinker. It was also a science in which exciting new discoveries were being made at the time. Physics deals with matter and energy and the interactions between the two. During World War II, while attempting to make the first atomic bombs, physicists had discovered how to split the atom. After the war ended in 1945, scientists began working on peaceful uses of atomic energy. There was also a new instrument called a computer that seemed to promise interesting developments in the future.

Mildred's most influential teacher at Hunter was Rosalyn Yalow, another of the scientists profiled in this book. Dr. Yalow encouraged her to pursue a career as a physicist and continued to follow her later accomplishments.

After graduating from college in 1951, Mildred was awarded a Fulbright Fellowship for graduate work in England. She studied for a year at Newnham, the women's college of Cambridge University. She then returned to the Radcliffe College in Cambridge, Massachusetts, where she earned a master's degree in 1952.

If she wanted to become a professional physicist—and she did by now—Mildred would need a Ph.D. Her academic record was so outstanding that she was able to get an appointment as a teaching assistant at the University of Chicago. She could teach part-time to support herself and do doctoral work in physics at the same time.

Some of her professors tried to discourage her from pursuing a career in research physics. They told her that most of the interesting problems in physics had already been solved, and that the ones that remained were "very difficult—too difficult for people like me" (Dresselhaus, "Perspectives on the Presidency of the American Physical Society," p. 38). Such challenges had never stopped her before; they simply made her work harder to prove herself.

Somehow she also found time to develop a relationship with a fellow student, Gene Dresselhaus, who became her husband shortly after the two of them received their Ph.D.s from the University of Chicago in 1958.

Both of them did their work in the general field of *solid-state physics*. All physical things in the universe can be found in three forms, or states: solid, liquid, and gaseous. At different temperatures, matter can change from one of these states to another. For example, water freezes into ice at 32° Fahrenheit. In a solid state, the atoms in a material are not free to move around as they do in the liquid and gaseous states, but they are locked into a regular pattern. Solid-state physics, then, deals with the study of solid materials.

Within this general area of physics, Gene Dresselhaus specialized in *semiconductors*. Many metals can conduct electrical current; that is, an electrical charge can pass through them. Benjamin Franklin's famous key-and-kite experiment showed that the metal key conducted the electrical charge from a bolt of lightning. Some metals are better conductors than others. In 1948, scientists learned how the atoms in silicon and certain other materials that arranged themselves in crystals could be used to transmit electricity. These semi-conductors, as they were called, made possible the invention of computers, transistor radios, and many other devices.

Mildred's work at the University of Chicago dealt with *superconductors*. Most substances that conduct electrical charges also have resistance to such charges. The resistance is expressed as heat. If one plugs too many high-voltage amplifiers into an electrical system that cannot handle that much power, the wires overheat and the system "fries." Resistance limits the amount of electrical power that can be used in any situation. But there are materials that lose all resistance when they become very cold. These materials are called superconductors. When cooled to absolute zero –459.67° (Fahrenheit) they allow an electrical charge to pass through without growing weaker, as it would in most materials. In fact, the charge grows stronger, because there is nothing to stop it. Little energy is required to start the current, and none at all to keep it going.

Superconductors are still in the experimental stage, but they hold great promise for future applications. They can be used to create lighter, more powerful magnets; to store electrical energy until it is needed; to design more efficient computers; and for many other uses not even foreseen today.

After graduation and their marriage, the young couple moved to Cornell University, where Gene Dresselhaus joined the faculty of the physics department. Mildred was able to do a year of postgraduate work under a National Science Foundation grant, and then their first child was born. The conventional thing for her to do would have been to settle down as a faculty wife and mother. It was the 1950s, a time when "career women" were considered unusual. But Mildred Dresselhaus was not a conventional person, and neither was her husband. They both wanted to be able to work in their chosen field. Mildred was well qualified for a teaching position, but Cornell had a rule against hiring both a husband and his wife. After two years at Cornell, they looked for jobs elsewhere.

Elsewhere turned out to be the Massachusetts Institute of Technology (MIT) back in Cambridge, Massachusetts. In 1960 both Gene and Mildred Dresselhaus were hired by MIT's Lincoln Laboratory, which at the time specialized in semiconductor research. Mildred was able to make the switch to semiconductor work because of her broad general background in physics. She could use much of what she had learned in working with superconductors in the new research. In addition to her activities at Lincoln Laboratory, she could work at MIT's Francis Bitter National Magnet Laboratory, a new center for research on magnetism. This laboratory could produce magnetism that was a hundred thousand times more powerful than the earth's natural magnetic field.

Since arriving there in 1960, Mildred Dresselhaus has continued to be associated with MIT as a research scientist and teacher. She has achieved a reputation as one of the world's leading scientists, not because of any one breakthrough or discovery, but because of a long series of contributions to human knowledge of materials and energy. She has worked mostly in what she calls "small science," day-to-day experimental work in which the connections among facts are not always clear and the practical applications not immediately considered.

Her work involves finding ways to change the structures of certain solids so that they become new materials that make possible new technologies. For example, she has researched the combining of very thin layers of graphite with layers of metal in a patterned framework called a *superlattice*. The arrangement and the proportions of metal and graphite can be varied to produce different results. Such new compounds allow scientists to study the behavior of magnetism in circumstances not found in nature. These studies also make it possible to design a device and then create in the laboratory the materials needed to build it.

Dresselhaus acts as a consultant to research and development experts in industry, helping them to put her discoveries to practical use. However, she says that most of the work of her group (herself, her graduate students, and co-workers) "is not on the applied level, though we do work on materials that have commercial interest. We tend to be ten years down the pike—ten years in advance of commercial applications" (Noble, p. 148).

Her accomplishments have been recognized through many promotions and honors. In 1967, MIT named her to the Abby Rockefeller Mauze chair as visiting professor in electrical engineering. She was made a full professor in 1968 and permanent holder of the Mauze chair in 1973. She has served as a visiting professor at universities in Brazil, Israel, Japan, and Venezuela and as an advisor to industries and government agencies.

Dresselhaus's skills go beyond the laboratory. An efficient administrator, she works well with people and is a good organizer. In 1972 she was named associate head of the department of electrical science and engineering at MIT, a post that she filled for two years. She has also been active on National Science Foundation committees and boards.

In 1981, Mildred Dresselhaus was asked to run for vice president of the American Physical Society, the national organization of professional physicists. She was surprised by the suggestion and felt sure that she would have little chance against the other nominee, a well-known male physicist. When she asked her boss at MIT about the possibility, he encouraged her to run for the office. However, he did not take her candidacy seriously enough to reduce her work assignments for the next four years.

Mildred Dresselhaus

Her platform urged APS to involve more younger members in its leadership, to sponsor more studies on important national issues, to support basic research, and to try to communicate better with the general public so that nonscientists could be more informed voters and citizens. Dresselhaus upset the other candidate and in 1982 took over as vice president of APS. After two years in that position, she was elected president.

She welcomed the chance to work with other prominent physicists and to learn about developments in many different areas of physics. In her years at MIT she "became more and more of an expert in an increasingly narrow field" (Dresselhaus, p. 38). Now she could see how her own work fit into a much broader framework. During her presidency, the society continued an international emphasis begun under her predecessor and conducted studies of such national issues as Strategic Defense Initiative ("Star Wars") and nuclear safety. With Hans Frauenfelder of the National Academy of Sciences, she held a briefing of George Keyworth, President Ronald Reagan's science advisor.

Busy as both of them were, Gene and Mildred Dresselhaus always made family an important priority in their lives. They raised four children. A nanny cared for the preschoolers during the daytime when both parents were at work. Evenings were family times. All the Dresselhauses enjoyed music, so Mildred supervised lessons on stringed instruments while Gene taught piano. When they were older, the children got to use such MIT facilities as the swimming pool and skating rink. They also traveled all over the world with their parents.

Having spent her life as one of only a few women in a field dominated by men, Mildred Dresselhaus had and continues to have a concern about the problems of women in science. When she started teaching solid state physics at MIT in the 1960s, there were few women in her classes. Those who were there sat silently, afraid to ask questions or take part in class discussions. Professor Dresselhaus noticed that, later, when the percentage of women students rose to between 10 percent and 15 percent, the women were willing to speak up. With other female faculty members, Dresselhaus started a Women's Forum at MIT, which helped to promote affirmative action policies there.

Problems still exist for women graduate students. Though they seem able to compete on an equal basis in the classroom, many have trouble in the lab. A survey conducted by Dresselhaus showed that women physics students tended to work harder, feel more pressure, and believe that they get less help than men do. In many other majors, women actually believed their work was worse than it was. Twenty percent of women graduate students in physics felt that their sex made it more difficult for them to succeed at MIT. Professor Dresselhaus says that women students tend to be afraid to take risks. Since most advances in science come through risk-taking, these women must be trained to be more independent.

Molecular models demonstrate some of Mildred Dresselhaus's work.
(Photo by Len Rubenstein)

Dresselhaus has had an enormous influence as a teacher at MIT. Her solid state physics class is so clear and well organized that in her early years at MIT, when she was still on a temporary appointment, students circulated a petition to keep her on the faculty. She is not only an outstanding classroom teacher but also makes herself available to students after hours, providing individual help and inviting groups of students to her home to discuss problems in science.

From 1977 to 1983, Dr. Dresselhaus was director of the Center for Materials Science and Engineering at MIT. In 1985, she was named in institute professor. This is the highest honor the school gives to its teachers, and only 12 faculty members can be designated institute professors at any one time. Dresselhaus was the first woman to be so honored.

Mildred Dresselhaus learned independence early. Perhaps it was those early hard times in Brooklyn that gave her the toughness she needed to succeed in a field where she was part of a small minority. She became not only an equal participant but a leader in international physics research, and she is still a prominent physicist after more than 30 years at MIT.

Asked what advice she would give to girls who were interested in a career in science, she said, "Follow your interests, get the best available education and training, set your sights high, be persistent, be flexible, keep your options open, accept help when offered, and be prepared to help others" (letter to the author). She believes that all women need is a chance to prove themselves. Her own career is the best testimony to the truth of that belief.

Chronology

November 11, 1930	Mildred Spiewak is born in New York City
1951	graduates from Hunter College; wins Fulbright fellowship to Cambridge, England
1952	earns master's degree at Radcliffe College
1958	earns Ph.D., University of Chicago; marries Gene Dresselhaus; receives post-doctoral fellowship at Cornell
1960	takes position at Lincoln Laboratory, Massachusetts Institute of Technology
1967	is appointed visiting professor in electrical engineering, MIT
1968	is named full professor at MIT
1972	becomes associate department head, electrical science and engineering, MIT
1973	is made permanent holder of Abby Rockefeller Mauze chair, MIT
1977	becomes director, Center for Materials Science and Engineering
1982	is elected vice president, American Physical Society
1984	is elected president, American Physical Society
1985	is named institute professor at MIT

Further Reading

Works by Dresselhaus

Dresselhaus, Mildred. "Perspectives on the Presidency of the American Physical Society." *Physics Today*, July, 1985, pp. 37–44. Some of this article would be too technical for students, but it does give Dresselhaus's thoughts on current issues in physics.

———. "Women Graduate Students." *Physics Today*, June, 1986, pp. 74–75. Describes a study conducted at MIT on the problems women students may have there.

Works About Dresselhaus

Merrill, Sam. "Women in Engineering." *Cosmopolitan*, April, 1976, pp. 162–174. This article includes brief biographies of Dresselhaus and three other women engineers, based on interviews.

Litwack, Georgia. "If You Go Into Science and Engineering, You Go In to Succeed." *Harvard Magazine*, January/February 1980, pp. 49–53. An article based on an interview of Dresselhaus.

Noble, Iris, *Contemporary Women Scientists of America*. New York: Julian Messner, 1979, pp. 138–151. Contains a readable and informative summary of Dresselhaus's life and career.

"Society Elects Mildred Dresselhaus Vice President." *Physics Today*, January, 1982, p. 91. This brief article shows how highly regarded Dresselhaus is in her profession.

Index

Boldface numbers indicate main headings

A

Accessory chromosome theory 22
Addams, Jane 43
Admiralty Islands 71
Adolescence 68–75
Albatross, The (boat) 96
Aliciella (flower) 1
American Association of Physicists in Medicine (AAPM) 54
American Cancer Society 53
American Fuchsia Society 9
American Men of Science (encyclopedia) 11
American Physical Society 122–123
American Radiation Society 51
American Samoa 68–70
American Society of Naturalists 22
Animal Mind, The (Washburn) x
Anthropology ix
  Mead 66–77
Antibodies 111
Antigen 111
Arapesh tribe 72
Arnold Arboretum 9
Arsenic 42
Ash Can Cats 68, 69
Astronomy ix
  Cannon 26–35
  Mitchell viii
Astrophysics 32
Atlantic Monthly (magazine) 94
Atomic bomb 52, 109, 119
Atomic Energy Commission (AEC) 52, 54

B

Bacteriology 39–40
Bakke, Allan 107
Bali 73
Banting, Frederick 59
Barnard College (New York City) 67
Bateson, Gregory 73
Bateson, Mary Catherine 73
Becquerel, Henri 110
Berson, Solomon A. 110–112
Biochemistry ix
Biology viii, x—*See also Genetics*
  molecular 86
Birth control 41
Boas, Franz 67
Botanical Congress, International 10–11

Botany ix
  Britton ix
  Eastwood 1–14
Boveri, Theodore 20
Brandegee, Katharine 6
Brandegee, Townsend Stith 6
Britton, Elizabeth ix
Bryn Mawr (Pennsylvania) College 19, 38
Burroughs, John 3

C

California, University of (UC) 49
California Academy of Sciences 1–2, 6, 12
California Botanical Club 9
California Institute of Technology (Caltech) 83
California Spring Blossom and Wildflower Association 9
Cancer
  pesticides and 101
  radiation physics 50–54
  research
    of Emerson ix
    of Quimby 50–54
    of Yalow 111
  RIA test 113
  thyroid research 111
Cancer Society, American—*See American Cancer Society*
Cannon, Annie Jump **26–35**
  childhood 26–27
  chronology 34
  classification system 30–32
  education 27–28
  further reading 35
  graduate study 29
  Henry Draper Catalog 31
  Nineteenth Amendment 31
  nova 31
  photography 29
  spectroscopy 28–31
  star gazing 26–27
  variable stars 30
Cannon, Mary Elizabeth Jump 26
Cannon, Wilson Lee 27
Cannon's system of classification 30–32
Carbohydrates 57–64, 59–65
Carbon monoxide 42
Carnegie Institute 20–21
Carson, Maria McLean 93, 99

Index

Carson, Rachel viii–ix, **92–105**
  childhood 93
  chronology 104
  DDT campaign 99–101
  Edge of the Sea 97–99
  education 93–94
  environmentalism 92–93, 99–103
  further reading 105
  Sea Around Us 96–97
  Under the Sea Wind 95
  Silent Spring 101–102
  writing career 94
Carson, Robert Warden 93
Chemical industry 101
Chien-Shiung Wu x
Chromosomes
  activator 86
  dissociator 86
  DNA 86, 88
  jumping genes 89
  mutations 83
  nucleolar organizer region 84
  research
    of McClintock 81–82
    of Stevens 20, 21
  ring chromosomes 83–84
  sister cells 86
  transposition theory 86–87
Clark, Eugenie ix
Cocaine 40–41
Cold Spring Harbor Laboratory (New York) 78–79, 85
Columbia University (New York City)
  atomic bomb research 52
  Mead 74
  Quimby 49, 54
  Yalow 108
Comets viii, 28
Coming of Age in Samoa (Mead) 70
Commoner, Barry 75
Computers 117, 119, 120
Conservation
  Eastwood 12
Constitution, United States
  nineteenth amendment 32
Cori, Carl F. 57–64
Cori, Carl Thomas 62
Cori, Gerty viii, **57–65**
  awards 57, 62
  carbohydrates research 59–60
  childhood 58
  chronology 64
  Cori cycle 61
  education 58
  enzymes research 60–61
  further reading 65
  insulin research 59–60
  metabolism research 59–61, 63
  Nobel Prize 62

  teaching career 58–59
  Yalow and 114
Cori cycle 61
Cori-ester—*See Glucose-1-phosphate*
Cornell University (Ithaca, New York)
  Dresselhaus 121
  McClintock 80–81
  Quimby 52
Cornish, Edward 43
Creighton, Harriet 83
Cressman, Luther 68, 70
Curie, Marie 48, 51, 108, 110
Curie, Pierre 48, 110
Curie-Joliot, Irene 48–49, 110
Cyanide 42
Cyclotron 52
Cytogenetics ix
Cytology 16, 81

D

Dangerous Trades, The (Oliver) 41
DDT 99–101, 102
Demerec, Milislav 85
Diabetes 59–65, 111
Dickens, Charles 3
Discrimination
  against Cori 58–59, 60
  Dresselhaus on 123–124
  in education vii
  equal rights amendment 44–45
  Quimby on 53
  in teaching 58–59, 60
  Yalow on 107
DNA (deoxyribonucleic acid) 86, 87
Draper, Henry 30
Dresselhaus, Gene 120–127
Dresselhaus, Mildred ix, x, **117–127**
  American Physical Society 122–123
  awards 122
  childhood 118
  chronology 126
  on discrimination 123–124
  education 118–120
  further reading 127
  MIT career 121–125
  motherhood 123
  semiconductors 120–121
  solid state physics 118–127
  superconductors 120–121
Drosophila (fruit fly) 81
Dunning, John R. 52

E

E. coli (bacterium) 86, 87
Eastwood, Alice ix, viii, **1–14**
  California Academy of Sciences 6–9
  childhood 2–3

Index

chronology 13
education 3
field research 4–5
further reading 14
herbarium 5–9
Hill tribe 7
San Francisco earthquake 1906 7–8
taxonomy 5–6
teaching career 3–4, 6–9
Eastwood, Colin Skinner 2
Eastwood, Eliza Gowdey 2
Eastwood, Kate 3
Eastwood, William 2–3
Eastwoodia (flower) 1
Ecology 92–93, 101
Edge of the Sea, The (Carson) 97–99
Electrical engineering ix
Emerson, Gladys Anderson ix
Emerson, Ralph Waldo 12
Enzymes 61
Equal Rights Amendment (ERA) 44–45
Exploring the Dangerous Trades (Hamilton) 44

F

Failla, Giaocchino 50, 51–52, 110
Fermi, Enrico 108
Fish and Wildlife Service, United States 95, 101
Fleming, Wiliamina 29
Flora of Colorado (book) 3
Fortune, Leo 70, 72
Franklin, Benjamin 120
Frauenfelder, Hans 123

G

Genes 81, 82
Genetics
  DNA 86, 87
  jumping genes 89
  linkage groups 82
  McClintock 78–91
  mutations 83
  nucleolar organizer region 84
  ring chromosomes 83–84
  Stevens 23
  transposition theory 78–79, 86–87
Genetics Society of America 88
Glucose 59
Glucose-1-phosphate 60
Glycogen 59, 63
Golden Gate Park (San Francisco, California) 8
Goldhaber, Gertrude 109
Goldhaber, Maurice 109
Graphite 122

Gray Herbarium 8
Grayia brandagei 5

H

Hamilton, Alice viii–ix, **36–47**
  bacteriology 39–40
  childhood 37
  chronology 46
  education 37–39
  equal rights amendment 44–45
  further reading 47
  Hull House 40–41, 43
  industrial diseases 42–43
  lead poisoning study 37, 41–42
  Occupational Disease Commission 41–42
  pathology 39–40
Hamilton, Allen 37
Hamilton, Edith 38
Hamilton, Gertrude Pond 37
Hammar, Frank 43
Handbook of the Trees of California, A (Eastwood) 8
Hargraves, M. M. 101
Harvard University (Cambridge, Massachusetts) 29, 30, 43
Henderson, Charles 41
Henry Draper Catalog (Cannon) 31
Henry Draper Extension (Cannon) 31
Herbarium 5–9, 6, 10
Higgins, Elmer 94
Hill Tribe, The 7
Hines, Bob 97–98
Hinkley, Arthur S. 49
Hinkley, Edith—*See Quimby, Edith*
Hopkins Seaside Laboratory (California) 18
Hormones 59
Houssay, Bernardo 62
Howe, Quincy 94
Howell, J. T(om) 10, 12
Huckins, Olga Owens 99
Hull House (Chicago, Illinois) 40, 43
Hunter College (New York City) 109, 119
Hyde, Helen x

I

Ichthyology
  Clark ix
Illinois, University of 108–109
Industrial Poisons in the United States (Hamilton) 43
Industry
  diseases related to 36–47
  safety measures 42
Insulin 59–65, 111
Iowa, University of vii
Isotopes 111

131

Index

J

Joliot, Frederick 110
Jumping genes 89

K

Keyworth, George 123
King, Helen Dean x
Kohler, Walter 43

L

Labor
industrial diseases 36–47
safety measures 42
Lead Institute, National—See National Lead
Institute
Lead poisoning 36–37, 41–42
Leaflets of Western Botany (magazine)
10
League of Women Voters 53
Linkage groups 82
Linnaeus, Carolus 10–11
Locksley Hall (poem) 93
Longworth, Alice Roosevelt 97

M

MacFarland, Dr. Frank Mace 18
Magnetic resonance imaging—See MRI
Magnets 121–122
Maize 81–82
Malay Archipelago (Wallace) 5
Manual of Botany of the Northern United
States (Coulter) 4
Manus tribe 71, 73–74
Massachusetts Institute of Technology
(MIT) (Cambridge) 121–125
McClintock, Barbara ix, x, **78–91**
awards 87, 88
childhood 79–80
chromosome research 82–91
chronology 90
at Cold Spring Harbor 85–91
education 80–81
further reading 91
jumping genes 89
mutation research 83–84
Nobel Prize 88
plant genetics 81–91
ring chromosomes theory 83–84
transposition theory 78–79, 86–
87
McClintock, Sara Handy 79–80
McClintock, Thomas Henry 79
Mead, Edward Sherwood 67
Mead, Margaret viii, **66–77**
adolescence studies 68–75
Ash Can Cats 68–69

childhood 67
chronology 76
Coming of Age in Samoa 70
criticism of 74
education 67–68
field research
American Samoa 68–70
Bali 73
New Guinea 71–72, 73–74
further reading 77
motherhood 73
National Food Habits Committee 73
teaching career 74
Medicine viii
cancer—See Cancer
Hamilton 36–47
industrial diseases 36–47
Quimby 50–54
Stevens 15–25
Taussig x
Yalow 110–116
Memorial Hospital for Cancer and Allied
Diseases (New York City) 50
Mendel, Gregor 81
Metabolism 57–65
Michigan, University of 38–39
Microscopes 16–17, 21, 81
Missouri, University of 83
Mitchell, Maria viii
Molecular biology—See Biology
Monod, Jacques 86
Morgan, Thomas Hunt 19–20, 21–23, 81,
83
MRI (magnetic resonance imaging) 114
Mundugumor tribe 72
Mutations 83
Myelofibrosis 62

N

National Academy of Sciences (NAS) 87
National Food Habits Committee 73
National Lead Institute 43
National Research Council (NRC) 83
National Science Foundation (NSF) 63
Naturalists, American Society of—See
American Society of Naturalists
New Guinea 71–73
New Yorker, The (magazine) 96, 101
Nineteenth Amendment 31
Nobel Prize
Cori 62
McClintock 88
Yalow x, 106, 112
Northwestern University (Evanston, Illinois)
40
Nova (type of star) 31
Nuclear energy 52, 113–114, 123—See also
Atomic bomb

Index

Nuclear physics—*See Physics*
Nucleolar organizer region (NOR) 84

O

Oberlin (Ohio) College vii
Occupational Accidents and Diseases, International Congress on 41
Occupational Disease Commission 41
Oliver, Sir Thomas 41
Omnibus (TV show) 99
O'Neill, Charles 41

P

Participant observation 68–69
Pathology 39–40, 59
Pesticides 99–101
Photography 29
Physical Society, American—*See American Physical Society*
Physicists in Medicine, American Association of—*See American Association of Physicists in Medicine*
Physics ix
  Dresselhaus 118–127
  nuclear physics x, 108–116
  Quimby 48–56
  radiation physics 48–56
  semiconductors 120–121
  solid state physics 118–127
  superconductors 120–121
  Yalow 108–116
Physiology
  Hyde x
Pickering, Edward C. 29–30, 31
Picric 43
Plumbism—*See Lead poisoning*
Popular Flora of Denver, A (Eastwood) 6
Porter, Robert 7
Prisms 28, 29
Proceedings of the National Academy of Sciences (journal) 83
Psychology
  Washburn x

Q

Quimby, Edith viii, x, **48–56**
  atom bomb 52
  awards 51, 54
  childhood 49
  chronology 55
  education 49
  further reading 56
  radiation 48–49
  radioactive sodium 52–53
  radiology 50–52
  research career 49–51

women's rights 53
  Yalow and 109
Quimby, Shirley L. 49

R

Radcliffe College (Cambridge, Massachusetts) 29
Radiation physics—*See Physics*
Radiation Society, American—*See American Radition Society*
Radioactive sodium 52
Radioactivity 108, 110
Radioimmunoassay (RIA) 111–113
Radioisotope 110
Radiology ix, 51–54, 110
Radios 120
Radium x, 50, 51
Radnitz, Gerty—*See Cori, Gerty*
Radnitz, Martha 58
Radnitz, Otto 58
Reader's Digest (magazine) 99, 101
Research Council, National—*See National Research Council*
Rhoades, Marcus 85
RIA test—*See Radioimmunoassay*
Ring chromosomes 83–84
Rocky Mountains 4
Rodell, Marie 96
Roentgen, Wilhelm 51
Roentgens 51
Romance Under the Waters (radio show) 94
Roosevelt, Theodore 97
Roswell Park Memorial Institute (Buffalo, New York) 59
Royal Astronomical Society 32

S

Samoa—*See American Samoa*
San Francisco earthquake 1906 7–8
Save-the-Redwoods League 9
Science (magazine) 8
Science Foundation, National—*See National Science Foundation*
Sciences, National Academy of—*See National Academy of Sciences*
Scott, Walter 3
Sea Around Us, The (Carson) 96, 97, 103
Semiconductors 120–121
Sex determination 15, 20–22
Shapley, Dr. Harlow 31
Sharp, Lester 81
Silent Spring (Carson) 94, 101–103
Sloan Jr., Alfred P. 54
Sloan-Kettering Institute for Cancer Research 54
Solid state physics—*See Physics*
Spectroscopy 28–31

Index

Spectrum 28
Spiewak, Mildred—*See Dresselhaus, Mildred*
SQUIDS (superconducting quantum interference devices) 117
Stadler, Lewis 84
Stanford University (Palo Alto, California) 18–19
Stare, Frederick T. 101
Stars—*See Astronomy*
Stevens, Emma Julia 16
Stevens, Ephraim 16
Stevens, Julia Adams 16
Stevens, Nettie Maria viii, **15–25**
 accessory chromosome theory 21–22
 Carnegie grant 20–21
 childhood 16
 chromosomes 20–22
 chronology 24
 education 16–19
 further reading 25
 graduate study 18–21
 McClintock and 81, 83
 microscope 17
 sex determination 15, 21–23
 teaching career 18
 X chromosome 21
 Y chromosome 21
Strategic Defense Initiative (SDI) 123
Studies in Spermatogenesis with Especial Reference to the Accessory Chromosome (paper) 22
Studies on Ciliate Infusoria (master's thesis) 18
Superconductors 120–121
Superlattice 122
Survey of Occupational Diseases, A (report) 42
Sussman, Clara 107
Sussman, Rosalyn—*See Yalow, Rosalyn*
Sussman, Simon 107

T

Taussig, Helen Brook x
Taxonomy 5–6, 12
Teach Your Child to Wonder (article) 103
Telescopes 29
Tenebrio molitor (type of worm) 21
Thoreau, Henry David 3
Thyroid gland disorders 111
Tiselius, Arne 63
Transposition theory 86, 87
Truman, Harry S. 63
Turpentine 42

U

Udall, Stewart 102
Undersea (article) 94

Under the Sea Wind (Carson) 95

V

Van Loon, Hendrik Willem 94

W

Wallace, Alfred Russel 5
Wallace, George J. 101
Wallace line 5
Washburn, Margaret Floy x
Washington University (St. Louis, Missouri) 60
Wellesley (Massachusetts) College 27–28
Westford Academy 16, 18
Wetherill, Al 5
White-Stevens, Robert 101
Whiting, Sarah F. 28
Whitman College (Walla Walla, Washington) 49, 52
Williams, Marian 94
Wilson, Carol 11
Wilson, Edmund Beecher 19–20, 21–22, 81
Wilson, Rosalind 97
Winthrop, Gov. John vii, x
World War II (1939-45) 52, 73

X

X chromosome 21
X rays 50, 83, 84

Y

Yale Review (journal) 96
Yalow, Aaron 108–109, 112
Yalow, Rosalyn ix, x, **106–116**
 awards 62
 Berson and 110–112
 childhood 107
 chronology 115
 Dresselhaus and 119
 education 107–109
 further reading 116
 motherhood 111
 Nobel Prize 106, 112
 nuclear physics 109–116
 Quimby and 49, 109–110
 radioimmunoassay 111–116
 RIA test 111–116
 thyroid research 111
Y chromosome 21

Z

Zoe (magazine) 6